# STAR WARS
# THE CLONE WARS
## LIGHTSABER DUELS
### PRIMA OFFICIAL GAME GUIDE

Written by:
Fernando Bueno

**Prima Games**
An Imprint of Random House, Inc.

3000 Lava Ridge Court, Suite 100
Roseville, CA 95661
www.primagames.com

The Prima Games logo is a registered trademark of Random House, Inc., registered in the United States and other countries. Primagames. com is a registered trademark of Random House, Inc., registered in the United States. Prima Games is an imprint of Random House, Inc.

Senior Product Manager: Donato Tica
Associate Product Manager: John Browning
Manufacturing: Stephanie Sanchez
Design & Layout: Calibre Grafix

**Acknowledgements**
Josh Heenan, Gavin Leung, Stephen Ervin, Rebecca Aghakhan-Mooshiabad, Don Meadows, Kev Harrison, Cai Jiahui.

All other trademarks are the property of their respective owners.

**Important:**
Prima Games has made every effort to determine that the information contained in this book is accurate. However, the publisher makes no warranty, either expressed or implied, as to the accuracy, effectiveness, or completeness of the material in this book; nor does the publisher assume liability for damages, either incidental or consequential, that may result from using the information in this book. The publisher cannot provide any additional information or support regarding gameplay, hints and strategies, or problems with hardware or software. Such questions should be directed to the support numbers provided by the game and/or device manufacturers as set forth in their documentation. Some game tricks require precise timing and may require repeated attempts before the desired result is achieved.

ISBN: 978-0-7615-6132-3
Library of Congress Catalog Card Number: 2008937618
Printed in the United States of America

08 09 10 11 LL 10 9 8 7 6 5 4 3 2 1

## CONTENTS

Fernando "Red Star" Bueno (aka dukkhah) has been a gamer since opening his first Atari, and has been writing creatively since his early years in high school. During college he combined his loves for gaming and writing and began freelancing for popular gaming websites. The San Diego native found his way to Northern California shortly after high school. After graduating from the University of California, Davis, with a dual degree in English and art history, he was able to land a job as an editor for Prima Games. Though happy with his position as an editor, his life called him to Las Vegas where he now resides. During the move to Nevada, he also made the move to author and has since written a number of game books, including *Naruto Uzumaki Chronicles 2*, *Prince of Persia: Two Thrones*, *Fight Night Round 3*, and *Stubbs the Zombie*.

In his time off he enjoys the works of Hermann Hesse, Johann Van Goethe, Franz Kafka, and EGM. When not writing for Prima, he continues to work on his craft as a poet.

We want to hear from you! E-mail comments and feedback to fbueno@primagames.com.

# DEDICATION

**This book and game are dedicated in memory of Ian Lovell, Lead Animator.**

# INTRODUCTION

## Acknowledgments

Aside from being one of the best friends a guy could have, Don Tica is one of the best people I could ever hope to work with. Of course, he's not without his Padawan, John Browning, who is just as cool a fella and a pleasure to work with. Thanks to them both for making my job easier.

Thanks also to all the great people and creative minds at LucasArts and Krome Studios. Without the Star Destroyer–sized wealth of support, this book wouldn't have gotten done.

## The Story up until Now...

Surely you've come to know the story of Anakin Skywalker, Jedi Master Yoda, Obi-Wan Kenobi, and the Jedi Order. You may even be familiar with the story of the Rebellion against the Empire or have heard whisperings of a dark organization named the Sith. But for those who need a reminder of where it all began, the following section provides all the background information needed to begin your adventure as you enlist in the Clone Wars.

## Star Wars: Episode I The Phantom Menace

During a time of turmoil in the Galactic Republic, a powerful organization known as the Trade Federation engaged in an aggressive maneuver to block trade routes to and from the planet Naboo. While the Congress of the Republic stalled on resolving the conflict, the Supreme Chancellor of the Republic secretly sent out two Jedi Knights to help resolve the issue quickly and quietly. Unfortunately, both the Jedi Knights and the people of Naboo were unaware that the Trade Federation was being secretly coerced into their actions by a more powerful dark force.

Upon arriving to meet with the Trade Federation delegates, the Jedi were ambushed and forced to flee. In their escape, they rescued Queen Amidala of Naboo and made a dash across the stars. As they fled, Qui-Gon Jinn, the elder of the two Jedi, came upon a small child with an extraordinarily high capacity for the Force—the energy that flows through all living things and that Jedi can harness into unique abilities. Convinced that the child, Anakin Skywalker, was the one prophesied to bring balance to the Force, Qui-Gon Jinn rescued him from slavery and took him on as an apprentice. It was not until after they met with the Jedi Council that Anakin's dark and troubled past was brought into question. Unmoved by the Council's warnings, Qui-Gon Jinn continued informally with Anakin's training.

As the Jedi fled from the Trade Federation with Queen Amidala, they found that they were being hunted by a dark figure highly skilled with a lightsaber and shrouded in the dark side of the Force. Upon hearing of the mysterious figure's attack on Qui-Gon Jinn, the Jedi Order realized that the Sith—a dark Order long thought to be extinct—was actually still active. Meanwhile, Senator Palpatine, a two-faced politician with dark ambitions, secretly and successfully schemed to overthrow the Supreme Chancellor and take his place.

In a final move of desperation, Senator Amidala (accompanied by Qui-Gon Jinn, Obi-Wan Kenobi, and Anakin Skywalker) fled back to Naboo to help liberate her planet from the Trade Federation. Though they were supposed to protect Amidala, the Jedi had a second motive for returning. They were to draw out the Dark Lord who attacked them earlier and reveal the existence of the Sith. In a final confrontation, Qui-Gon Jinn exposed and was defeated by the Sith Lord Darth Maul, who was in turn defeated by Obi-Wan Kenobi. In the end, Palpatine became the new Supreme Chancellor and took control of the Republic, Naboo was liberated from the Trade Federation, Obi-Wan honored Qui-Gon Jinn's final request and took Anakin as his Padawan learner, and the Sith were exposed.

But a question remained: If Darth Maul was a Sith Lord, was he a student or a master?

## Star Wars: Episode II Attack of the Clones

Ten years after the reemergence of the Sith, Obi-Wan Kenobi, Anakin Skywalker, and the rest of the Jedi Knights struggled to keep order in the galaxy. Several thousand solar systems threatened to leave the Republic as they followed a Separatist movement led by the mysterious Count Dooku, a former Jedi Knight. Senator Amidala of Naboo, the former queen, returned to the Galactic Senate to petition for the creation of a Republic army to aid the struggling Jedi. Unfortunately, not everyone shared in her vision, as she was under the repeated threat of assassination.

After another failed assassination attempt on Amidala, the Jedi Order assigned Obi-Wan and Anakin, whom she'd not seen in years, as her personal bodyguards. While they were on assignment, Anakin's impetuous nature got the better of him, and he used the Senator as bait to draw out her assassin. Still, Amidala's would-be assassin would not relent. She struck once again while Amidala was under the watchful eye of the two Jedi, and the duo chased the assassin down. When they caught her, she was killed by a poisoned dart before she could reveal the name of the person who issued her orders.

While Obi-Wan followed the trail of clues back to a bounty hunter named Jango Fett, Anakin was assigned to protect Senator Amidala while in seclusion on Naboo. The trail to Jango Fett led Obi-Wan to the mysterious planet Kamino. There he found a race of cloners with an army of soldiers they claimed was commissioned by Jedi Master Sifo-Dyas, who had died over ten years prior. Though he was perplexed by the development, Obi-Wan didn't have much time to mull it over, as Jango Fett attacked him unsuccessfully before fleeing the planet.

Meanwhile, Anakin and Amidala grew closer while in seclusion. Though Anakin was haunted by the memory of his mother, his love for Amidala grew every day they spent together. Eventually, Anakin's concerns about his mother overwhelmed him, and he was drawn away from the hideout in Naboo. With Amidala in tow, Anakin set out in search of his mother only to find that she'd been captured by a Tusken Raider hunting party.

In a failed attempt to rescue his mother, Anakin was briefly reunited with her long enough for her to die in his arms. In a fit of rage, he single-handedly destroyed the entire village of Tusken Raiders. Meanwhile, Jango Fett led Obi-Wan to the Trade Federation planet Geonosis. There, lying amidst a large concentration of Federation ships, was a large battle droid factory. Obi-Wan infiltrated the factory to discover Count Dooku and his followers secretly scheming to destroy the Jedi and overthrow the Republic.

Before he was captured, Obi-Wan sent out a call to Anakin and the Jedi Order. However, instead of following the Jedi Order's instructions to protect Amidala on Naboo, Anakin and Amidala went in search of Obi-Wan in hopes of rescuing him. When Anakin and Amidala arrived at Geonosis, they, too, were captured by Dooku's troops. Meanwhile, Supreme Chancellor Palpatine issued orders to create a grand army of the Republic, knowing full well that the army was waiting for him on Kamino. When the Jedi arrived on Geonosis to rescue Obi-Wan, they found that not only was he in danger, but so were Anakin and Amidala. The battle on Geonosis was short but fierce. Just as the Jedi's numbers began to dwindle and all hope seemed to fade, Master Yoda arrived with an army of stormtroopers.

Upon seeing Jedi Master Mace Windu defeat his loyal soldier Jango Fett, Count Dooku fled. Anakin and Obi-Wan followed Dooku and cornered him in a cave where the two Jedi engaged the traitorous count in heated battle. Dooku's skills were far superior, and he was able to fell Obi-Wan and sever Anakin's arm. Just as Dooku was about to destroy Anakin once and for all, Yoda arrived and rescued the two fallen Jedi. Foiled by his former master, Dooku fled once again—this time successfully.

Though he got away, Dooku did inadvertently reveal that a mysterious Darth Sidious was somehow controlling the Senate. Anakin and Amidala secretly married, but the damage had been done. Anakin had already taken his first step toward the dark side. The dark side of the Force grew stronger, and the Clone Wars began.

# The Clone Wars

The Clone Wars spanned about three years and rapidly spread throughout the galaxy after the Battle of Geonosis. Though Count Dooku seemed the public mastermind of the Separatist strategy, he secretly answered to his Sith Master, Darth Sidious. Military actions were led by the cyborg General Grievous, and Dooku had a cadre of specialized underlings, including the bounty hunter Durge and the dark side warrior Asajj Ventress. Early in the war, Dooku's forces mined the hyperspace routes that connected the Core Worlds to the rest of the galaxy, effectively cutting off the Republic from the bulk of its resources and allowing the Separatists relative freedom of movement in the Outer Rim. To match this maneuver, the Jedi entreated the Hutts to share their control of the Outer Rim, allowing the Republic to move their vessels through Hutt-controlled space.

Over the course of the war, public opinion of the Jedi Order waxed and waned. Their early defeats underscored their vulnerability, and their reluctant adoption of the rank of general caused them to be blamed for many of the missteps in the Clone Wars. Still, there emerged champions like Anakin Skywalker and Obi-Wan Kenobi, respectively dubbed the Hero with No Fear and the Negotiator by an approving public. Heroes arose similarly on the side of the Separatists.

# Lightsaber Duels and Jedi Alliance

And it is during these perilous times that we begin our adventure. You may know the inevitable outcome of Sidious and the Empire—how the rise of a young Jedi named Luke Skywalker was the demise of Darth Vader and his master, Lord Sidious. But how were the Jedi able to curry the favor of the scoundrel Jabba and the Hutts during the Clone Wars?

Prepare, for it is during these dark days that our adventure will take place. But first you must know the ways of the Force....

# How to Use This Book

| TIP |
| --- |

Whenever you see one of these Tip boxes, stop and meditate on the information contained within. These boxes provide tidbits of information that help you increase your abilities, improve as a duelist, and often enhance your experience overall.

## NOTE

Notes are supplementary bits of info that may not enhance your abilities or experience, but will provide info on the game or the book. You can live without these, but if you thirst for knowledge, read them.

## CAUTION

Other boxes may make you a better duelist or a notch smarter, but only Caution boxes will keep you alive. The sole purpose of these boxes is to provide you vital warnings of dangers that lay ahead.

## HEALTH TRIGGERED EVENT

Sidebars like these will often contain different types of supplemental information. In the Challenge section of "A Duelist's Profile," for example, it will detail background info on the challenge at hand.

# A Duelist's Profile

We've organized this book as efficiently as possible. So while introductory chapters like this and the Modes chapter may have a brief synopsis of what to expect from the book or the game, the real bulk of the information is provided in the "A Duelist's Profile" section. There you will find everything from signature combos to beating Challenge and Battle mode fights!

**Character Bio:** This section has all the information about your chosen duelist's background and their physical appearance. Usually, a fighter's bio will provide you a small glimpse behind their reason for fighting.

**Stats:** This table shows a fighter's strengths and weaknesses. Ratings range from 0 (weakest) to 5 (strongest).

**Costumes:** Check out your chosen one's optional costumes! Alternate costumes are purely cosmetic but are tons of fun to unlock!

**Fighting Style:** A short description of your duelist's fighting style provides great info on their combative tendencies and helps you know how to handle them in combat. This information is great playing as and against a particular fighter!

**Combo Table:** The combo table details all five of a fighter's signature combos. The letters in the table refer to Wii Remote actions: U is for Upward swing, D is for Downward swing, L is for Left swing, R is for Right swing, and S is for Stabbing. Diagonal motions don't correspond to any kind of attack, so keep your motions clear and concise. But more on that in the controls chapter.

**Challenge Boxes:** These boxes contain everything on a particular task in Challenge mode. Everything from opponent, arena, and challenge requirement is listed here.

**Motivation Boxes:** These boxes provide a glimpse into the motivation behind a particular challenge. After all, the Jedi don't fight just to fight. Everything has a purpose.

**Challenge Strategy:** The text and accompanying screens in the Challenge section tell you everything you need to know on how to successfully complete the listed challenge. Mind you, there are several ways to accomplish a task, but the methods detailed in this section are proven to be successful.

**Battle Mode:** Battle mode fights are not restricted with specific tasks. The strategies in the Battle Mode section of a fighter's profile detail proven ways to defeat every opponent.

# Campaign Walkthrough

In Campaign mode, you participate in many key and side battles. Because the battles in Campaign mode are predetermined, you will often take control of either Ahsoka Tano, Obi-Wan Kenobi, or Anakin Skywalker. Each of the key battles in Campaign mode are broken down round by round to provide detailed strategy on how to emerge victorious through the Clone Wars.

**Breaking News:** Like the Motivation boxes in a duelist's profile, the Breaking News section provides information on the events leading up to the battle.

**The Duelists:** The combatant on the left is always the player-controlled character. Your opponent is on the right. Check the Stat boxes below to see how they match up!

**Round 1 and Round 2 Strategy:** This is strategy for each round of every fight! Everything from strategy on how to fight to the events happening between and after the fight are covered.

**Health Triggered Event Boxes:**
These boxes provide information on environmental effects that are triggered by your or the opponent's health. Sometimes these events are purely for entertainment. More often than not, they are environmental hazards that can either help or hinder you, so read these boxes to know what you're in for!

# MODES

Many of the modes detailed below vary in difficulty, which you choose at the game's beginning. However, some modes require that you select a particular difficulty setting in order to unlock certain challenges. Difficulty settings, from easiest to hardest, are Youngling, Padawan, Jedi Knight, and Grand Master.

# Campaign Mode

In Campaign mode, you play through several key battles from *The Clone Wars*. Because the events of the Clone Wars are prescripted, you are restricted to playing as either Anakin Skywalker, Obi-Wan Kenobi, or Ahsoka Tano. As you progress, you will unlock different chapters in the Clone Wars story. Once unlocked, you could come back and either play any previously unlocked chapter or pick up where you left off. The battles in Campaign mode have no time limits or restrictions, so take your time and enjoy being a hero of the Clone Wars.

# Challenge Mode

In the unique Challenge mode, you are tasked with completing certain tasks in a series of four duels. Fight challenges range from simply defeating your opponent within a time limit to performing several combos before defeating the enemy. After selecting Challenge mode, choose your fighter, then cycle through his or her four challenges. In order to attempt a Challenge, you must first meet the difficulty requirement. Some fighters' challenges may only be played at Grand Master difficulty, while others are playable at Padawan.

**TIP**

Check the "Secret Jedi Scrolls" chapter to find out how to unlock all of the Challenges for every fighter!

# Battle Mode

Like Campaign mode, the fights in Battle mode are prede-termined. That means that, depending on your chosen fighter, his or her opponents will be chosen for you. Unlike Campaign mode, these fights don't follow the Clone Wars plot but instead create unique matchups depending on the fighter. If you stop halfway through Battle mode, you won't be able to pick up where you left off. Consider Battle mode a six-fight test of endurance. There are no time limits, special requirements, or restrictions on these fights, so simply do your best and beat your opponent.

**NOTE**

Unlike Challenge mode fights, these duels aren't locked to any one difficulty. You can complete Battle mode on any difficulty you choose.

# Free Play Mode

In Free Play mode, you can play whatever you choose. After selecting your fighter, you can select your opponent and the arena in which to duel. Though there are no specific tasks to complete other than to defeat your selected opponent, Free Play mode is a perfect way to practice your skills. If you're having trouble defeating an opponent in a different mode, come to Free Play mode to re-create the challenge and practice! You can choose this mode in single-player and multiplayer.

**NOTE**

The fight difficulty is determined by whichever difficulty you choose at the start of your game.

# Quick Play Mode

In Quick Play mode, you are thrown into a fight without having to make any choices. After selecting Quick Play, your fighter, opponent, and the arena are chosen for you. Though the loading screen does offer you a hint of which fighter you might be using, the best part about Quick Play is that you don't know what lies ahead. That forces you to practice your skills with any duelist in any arena! This mode can be chosen in single-player and multiplayer.

# THE WAY OF THE SABER

## HUD (Heads Up Display) and Basic Controls

While Campaign mode has a very useful tutorial, the following pages will cover everything from basic controls to advanced combat techniques.

**Force Gauge:** The hexagon bars surrounding your fighter icon are your Force Gauge. By successfully parrying blows, hitting an opponent with Force-thrown objects, or landing combos, you fill each of the six bars that make up the gauge. Once it is full, you can unleash your Charged Combo. If you miss with the Charged Combo, the sixth bar will empty and you'll have to refill it again for another attempt at a Charged Combo.

**Force Energy:** This Force Energy can be spent on attacks such as Force Throw and Force Lightsaber Attacks. Your Force Energy slowly refills over time, but you can refill it more quickly by successfully landing blows on your opponent.

**Current Move:** This displays the name of your current move.

**Previous Move:** This displays the name of your previous move.

Smash Attack
Charged Combo Ready

**Health:** The green bar measures your health. Once completely depleted, you are defeated. If you are defeated once, the green bar becomes orange. After it is depleted a second time, you lose the duel.

## Movement

| Action | Control |
|--------|---------|
| Move | ○ |

To move about the arena, press ○ in the direction you want to move. When moving toward your enemy, your fighter will always run. When backing away, your fighter will cautiously step backward, keeping his or her eyes locked on the opponent. Pressing up and down on the control stick (○), however, will move your duelist farther into the background or closer in the foreground of the arena. Keep this in mind as you fight, because your movement and the corresponding actions on the control stick will change depending on which direction you are facing and where your opponent is located.

For example, if you're deep in the arena and the opponent has his back to the screen while standing in the foreground, then pressing ◁ or ▷ will move your fighter left or right in the background. If you wanted to walk toward your opponent in the foreground, press ▽. Similarly, if you're in the foreground and your enemy is in the background, press △ to move toward him rather than sidestepping left or right.

# Evade and Leaping Slash

| Action | Control |
|---|---|
| Backflip | ◎ (away from the enemy), Ⓐ |
| Forward flip | ◎ (toward the enemy), Ⓐ |
| Sidestep or evasive roll | ◎ (to your left or right), Ⓐ |
| Leaping Slash | ◎ (toward the enemy), Ⓐ, then downward slash as you land |

Pressing Ⓐ by itself will perform an evasive backflip. But by using Ⓐ in conjunction with the control stick (◎), you can perform a series of evasive maneuvers around the arena. Learn to combine your movement with the Evade button to deftly outmaneuver your opponent in battle. Evasive maneuvers allow you to dodge attacks and circumvent an enemy's defense and attack.

Evasive maneuvers require that you use the control stick, so they're governed by the same rules as basic movement. That means that left and right aren't always going to move you forward and backward, so keep in mind the direction you're facing when attempting to dodge. One of your most useful attacks is a Leaping Slash. By combining a downward slash attack with an evasive forward leap, you can dodge an enemy's attack and deliver a blow as you land behind them!

# Block and Parry

| Action | Control |
|---|---|
| Block | Hold Ⓑ |
| Parry | Hold Ⓑ then swing the Wii Remote in the opposite direction of the attack at the moment of impact |

Perhaps no skills are more undervalued in lightsaber dueling than blocking and parrying. Fledgling fighters often take a brash, undisciplined approach to lightsaber combat and either forget, or intentionally ignore, the defensive aspects of battle. Seasoned warriors, on the other hand, know that blocking and parrying often mean the difference between victory or defeat. To block, hold Ⓑ before your opponent delivers a blow. The incoming blow will often glance off your 'saber harmlessly. Keep in mind that blocking an attack deals a small amount of damage, and that the third blocked hit in a combo string will break a character's block, opening them up for the next strike.

A slightly more advanced technique, and one that you should always try to employ during battle, is to parry. Parrying begins like blocking, but it requires that you perform a counter-lightsaber swing in the opposite direction as the incoming attack. So if your opponent attacks with a left sideways slash, parry by blocking and swinging your Wii Remote in a right sideways slash at the moment of impact. If you're one second too late or too early, you might still block, but you'll fail to parry.

# Lightsaber Attack

The basics of combat are easy to learn—simply swing the Wii Remote in the direction you want to attack. However, using the basics to string together combos and formulate your own fighting style is another matter. At first it may seem as if your choices are limited, because there are only five different types of slash attacks (swinging the Wii Remote diagonally won't attack). In true Jedi form, though, lightsaber combat is kept from being overly and needlessly complicated. These five attacks are all you need.

| Action | Control |
|---|---|
| Left slash (light attack) | Swing the Wii Remote left |
| Right slash (light attack) | Swing the Wii Remote right |
| Upward slash (medium attack) | Swing the Wii Remote upward |
| Downward slash (medium attack) | Swing the Wii Remote downward |
| Stab (lunge) (heavy attack) | Thrust the Wii Remote forward (as if poking the air) |

To perform these attacks, keep your hand steady and make long sweeping movements with the Wii Remote. A flick of the wrist is all you may need at times, but if you're not precise, you may accidentally perform other attacks when you reset your hand to its most comfortable position. For example, if you start by moving from left to right, your hand will end in a position just right of where it started. Your instinct will be to move your hand back to its original position—back left—and you'll perform a left slash attack when you might have wanted to follow up with an upward swing. By using longer sweeping motions, you can string together more precise combos. You don't need to swing the Wii Remote across your body; just swing it enough so that your natural wrist movement doesn't complicate things for you.

**NOTE**

After you become accustomed to lightsaber combat, you may be able to shorten the length of your swing.

# Force Attacks and Charged Combos

Force attacks or Force-imbued attacks are similar to normal 'saber slashes with one mighty exception—they're imbued with the power of the Force. That makes Force Lightsaber attacks substantially more powerful than normal attacks. You can only perform Force-imbued attacks when you have Force Energy to spend.

| Action | Control |
|---|---|
| Force sideways slash | Hold Ⓩ then swing the Wii Remote left or right |
| Force upward slash | Hold Ⓩ then swing the Wii Remote upward |
| Smash attack | Hold Ⓩ then swing the Wii Remote downward |
| Force Thrust | Hold Ⓩ, then thrust the Wii Remote forward |
| Charged Combo | Once your Force Gauge is full, hold Ⓩ then swing the Wii Remote |

Furthermore, the damage inflicted by Force Lightsaber attacks depends on the amount of Force Energy you have. If your Force Energy bar is full, your Force Attacks will be more powerful than if it was low.

Use these attacks in between combos to spin your enemy around, slam them to the ground, or even knock them off the arena floor. These are some of the most useful attacks in any fighter's repertoire, so make frequent and smart use of them.

Charged Combos are special combos that you can use only after you've filled your Force Gauge. Once all six bars in the gauge are full, execute a Charged Combo to inflict major damage on your opponent.

# Special Attacks

| Action | Control |
|---|---|
| Special Attack | Hold Ⓩ, then thrust Nunchuk forward |

Every fighter has a special attack. As long as the fighter has Force Energy, they can focus the Force, then unleash it in their own special way. Obi-Wan Kenobi, for example, can perform a devastating Force Blast that knocks the target back and off their feet. If his Force Energy bar is full, his Force Blast will inflict major damage. If the Force Energy is low, then the blast might only nudge the enemy.

Some fighters who lack Force Energy, like Grievous or the EG-05 Jedi hunter droid for example, may not need it to perform their attacks. Instead, they use mechanical skill to perform a special attack. The EG-05 droid's special attack is a bolt of blaster fire from its palm!

**NOTE**

Each fighter's special attack is listed in the Stats table of their profile in the Duelists chapter.

# Force Throw

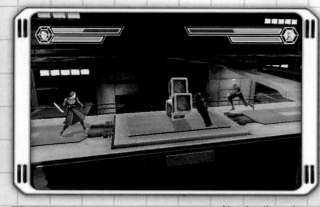

| Action | Control |
|---|---|
| Force Throw | Hold Ⓒ, then flick Nunchuk |

Nearly all combatants can use the Force to Force Throw objects. In every battle arena, there are several pieces of debris lying around. Hold Ⓒ to pick up an object, then flick the Nunchuk in the enemy's direction to hurl it at them. Force Thrown objects knock your enemy off balance and off their guard, while simultaneously charging your Force Gauge. While you need to have a minimum amount of Force Energy to Force Throw an object, the amount of Force Energy you have doesn't affect the damage done to your opponent.

Of course, that also means that fighters like General Grievous or the EG-05 Jedi hunter droid who lack Force Energy cannot execute Force Throws. While using the droid duelists, however, you can simulate Force Throwing by getting next to a tall, destructible object and using a sideways slash to cut the object and hurl it at your opponent.

# Advanced Combat Techniques

With the basics of combat down, you're ready to learn some advanced combat techniques. The following duel strategies will help you become one of the most powerful Jedi (or Sith) you can be.

## Combo Technique

The lightsaber arts are easy to pick up but require lots of practice to master. Part of becoming a great duelist is knowing how to execute proper combos. For the following lesson, we will examine Anakin Skywalker's Determined Assault combo. To execute this, you must swing the Wii Remote in the following pattern: right, down, left, then up. Imagine that you are drawing a square with the Wii Remote in a clockwise formation. Otherwise, whether you realize it or not, your combo will be as follows: right, recenter, down, recenter, left, recenter, then up. For every time that you recenter (or reposition) your hand, you're adding unwanted Wii Remote movement and potentially ruining the combo.

We've touched on this a bit in the Lightsaber Attacks section, but the importance of proper combo execution is paramount! If you constantly recenter your hand, you'll often execute unwanted attacks midcombo. That is not to say that you shouldn't recenter your hand position to a comfortable place, but do so only after executing a combo. Think of a combo as its own separate action during a fight, and string them together with shorter two- and three-hit combos.

## Circumvent the Defense

No plan of attack is effective if your blows don't hit their mark. To make sure you can successfully dish out some damage, you'll often have to break through or circumvent an opponent's defenses. Fighters like Count Dooku are exceptionally skilled at defensive techniques and can often drag out a match until its in their favor. Luckily there are a few techniques at your disposal for breaking through an enemy's defense. The first and most effective way is to use Stabbing (or lunging) attacks. Thrust the Wii Remote forward while an enemy's guard is up and you'll greatly increase the chances of knocking them off balance and pushing through their block.

Another is to use leaping slashes and Force Thrown objects to get around their defense. As the enemy carefully stalks around the arena with their guard up, use leaping slashes to jump over their defense and slash at their weak side. The blow will simultaneously get around the block and knock them to the ground. Force Thrown objects can work in a similar manner. Instead of rushing around or busting through an enemy's defense, use objects as a lead-in to the attack. By Force Throwing an object at the enemy's rear or flank, you can knock them off balance and create an opportunity to strike. Of course, if the object hits the enemy's sword, all is for nought, so make sure you're hitting an unprotected side.

 **TIP**

Sideways Force attacks are also great for spinning enemies around and exposing their weak side.

# Be Mindful of the Environment

# Be One with the Arena

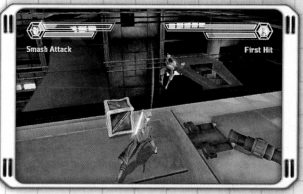

Nearly every environment has at least one environmental hazard that you can use to your advantage. While battling in the Droid Lab, several electrical conductors will often release dangerous currents of energy that can simultaneously stun an enemy and zap their health. Learn the environments so you can detect these hazards and be better prepared during combat. By learning to recognize certain cues, you can maneuver your enemy into position and let the hazard fall on them.

Each arena is different, so read the "Battlegrounds" chapter to learn more about each. And be forewarned: the hazards can hurt you as well....

Certain arenas are perched high above a dangerous location. Whether it be a Sarlacc pit or the molten lava of the Mustafar landscape that lies far below an arena, no fighter wants to be knocked off. Use Smash attacks to fling your foe off the arena and inflict some damage. The real fun doesn't begin, though, until they recover from the blow and leap back onto the main arena. After knocking them off, back away from the edge and give them space to return. Usually they'll return with a downward slash in hopes of exacting some small amount of revenge. When their attack misses, they're vulnerable to a follow-up attack. Act quickly—rush in while they're vulnerable and strike with a combo!

Knocking enemies off the arena can also be used as a defensive measure. If you're running low on health and need to create some breathing room, stay out of reach of the enemy's 'saber and use Smash attacks to knock them off the platform. One or two Smash attacks can be the difference between losing a match and a come-from-behind victory.

# BATTLEGROUNDS

## NOTE

Various levels have Health Triggered Events. These events can be anything from environmental hazards to those that happen in the background for entertainment value only.

## The Resolute

The main hangar of Anakin Skywalker's Venator Star Destroyer, the Resolute, becomes a makeshift arena as the Y-wing squadron prepares for battle.

## First Round

The Resolute is a small, medium-sized battle arena. There are no environmental hazards, but the various boxes and ship parts scattered about make this a great arena for someone with a high Force Energy rating. These fighters can Force Throw the projectiles and quickly fill their Force Gauge.

## NOTE

There is only one area for fighting on the Resolute, so both rounds take place on the hangar. There are no Health Triggered Events in this arena.

## Teth Castle Dungeon

Situated atop a mesa overlooking the Teth jungle, there is a seemingly abandoned monastery.

## First Round

The first round of battle in the Teth Castle Dungeon takes place on the dungeon's top level. There, the arena can be split into two areas, the foreground with several pieces of debris and the raised background. The multitiered environment is better suited for fighters with good Force Energy and Agility ratings.

## HEALTH TRIGGERED EVENT

If a Jedi player is reduced to 75 percent health, super battle droids enter the fray through the rear grate. If a Sith or Sith minion player is reduced to 75 percent health, clones enter the fray through the rear grate. These events are mutually exclusive; if one is triggered, the other will not be.

# Second and Third Rounds

The second and third rounds of battle in the Teth Castle Dungeon take place in the dark and dank depths of the rancor pit! This is a medium-sized arena with a decent amount of depth. There are no raised or tiered areas on which to fight, but the many rancor beast bones lying around make it a great place for fighters who have high Force Energy ratings.

## HEALTH TRIGGERED EVENT

If a Jedi player is reduced to 90 percent health, battle droids emerge to battle the rancor in the background. If any Sith or Sith minion player is reduced to 90 percent health, clones emerge to battle the rancor. These events are mutually exclusive; if one is triggered, the other will not be.

# Teth Castle Ramparts

The shadowy chamber of the abandoned monastery leads to the stone bridge high above the clouds.

## First Round

The first round of battle in the Teth Castle Ramparts takes place inside the large, circular castle tower. The wide-open area is perfect for combo technicians and speedy combatants. The room is so large that it makes speedy fighters harder to catch and gives duelists with high Combo ratings enough room to move around and develop their attacks. Since there is significantly less debris lying around this area than in others, fighters can still use Force Thrown projectiles but might meet with less success since the target has more room to dodge and projectiles might have to travel longer distances.

## HEALTH TRIGGERED EVENT

If either player is reduced to 75 percent health, the door at the arena's rear will open and a battle will take place between the clones and the droids.

# Second and Third Rounds

Unlike the wide-open area of the rampart tower, the bridge is a slightly smaller and restrictive space. This accommodates duelists who excel in close-quarter combat and who have higher Force Attack ratings. With a high Force Attack rating, a fighter can inflict more damage with shorter, quicker attacks. Fighters can also use Smash attacks and strong combos to knock enemies off the bridge on the far left.

## HEALTH TRIGGERED EVENT

If either player is reduced to 90 percent health, a vulture droid will come screaming out of nowhere, crashing into the bridge and smashing off a large section that falls into the abyss. If a Jedi player is reduced to 75 percent health, the Twilight will fly past in the background under fire from a horde of vulture droids. If a Sith or Sith minion player is reduced to 75 percent health, the Twilight will fly past, attacking several vulture droids. It eventually will zoom past the arena and release a big pile of crates from its cargo hold, destroying the pursuing vulture droids. When either player is reduced to 50 percent health, a mighty Venator will begin to pass over the level.

# Tatooine Dune Sea

On a bleak, barren region of the desert planet Tatooine, known as the Dune Sea, a battle takes place amongst the bones of Krayt Dragons and ancient ruins.

## First Round

The first-round arena is surprisingly complex for a desert. This large area is littered with Krayt bones to use as projectiles, and even fighters with no capacity for the Force can hurl the teeth on the arena's far left. On occasion, a small transport shuttle will zip by overhead and leave a short sand wake that can disrupt combat. If you time it just right, you can use the small sandstorms to interrupt your opponent's attacks.

## HEALTH TRIGGERED EVENT

If a Jedi player is reduced to 50 percent health, several vulture droids will perform a flyby and a gunship will crash into the ruins in the background. If a Sith or Sith minion player is reduced to 35 percent health, then three gunships will fly in the background over the arena, firing missiles as they go.

# Second and Third Rounds

The secondary area of the Tatooine arena is a long walkway inside the desert ruins. As the battle begins, several large spherical stones will drop from above. For a gifted fighter, they're perfect projectiles. On the arena's far right, several droid soldiers open fire into the main walkway, creating a small diversion near the arena's right. The long walkway is great for fighters gifted with strong combo skills.

### HEALTH TRIGGERED EVENT

If a Jedi player is reduced to 75 percent health, a gunship will crash in the background at center stage. If a Jedi player is reduced to 55 percent health, two vulture droids will do flybys.

If a Sith or Sith minion player is reduced to 80 percent health, a vulture droid will crash into the background on the left-hand side, destroying a group of battle droids. If a Sith or Sith minion player is reduced to 55 percent health, a gunship will descend into the background, fire at some battle droids, then exit (this event loops). Also, a vulture droid will perform a flyby from left to right.

# Separatist Listening Post

On one of the Three Sister Moons of Ruusan, a giant sky station floats in the skies above the surface, serving as a communications center for the Separatists.

## First Round

The Separatist Listening Post is a crescent-shaped arena abuzz with activity. While the arena is free from environmental hazards and debris, the background is often the picture of turmoil. When fighting on the Listening Post, keep a close eye on the floor panels. Once broken, they periodically explode in short bursts of electricity. Stepping on them won't hurt you, but the electrical charge might slow you down a step. There are very few objects to throw, so this arena, like the Teth Castle Rampart bridge, is great for fighters who excel in close-quarter combat.

### HEALTH TRIGGERED EVENT

Each Health Triggered Event will play only once and will not trigger until the previous event has played out, so if you trigger one event quickly, you might miss out on seeing all the events. Once either player gets reduced to 90 percent health, the gunship parked on the level's left side takes some laser fire and explodes. When either player is at 80 percent health, a gunship will fly in and land on the right platform, where it drops four clones that proceed to the main background platform and start firing on the droids in the distance. Once either player gets reduced to 70 percent health, a vulture droid careens out of control from the left and collides with the large radar dish on the sky station, causing the dish to detach and pass over the arena dropping debris.

Once either player gets reduced to 60 percent health, the gunships hovering in the background will fire several missiles that destroy all the droids; then they explode and fall out of sight. Once either fighter loses 50 percent health, the Twilight takes off and R2-D2 and Goldie come down to the platform in the background and begin fighting. At 40 percent health, Yoda and some clones will do a quick flyby at the front of the level.

# Second and Third Rounds

First Hit

During the second and third rounds, the Separatist Listening Post becomes unstable and begins to fall out of the sky! Explosions erupt everywhere, and the level begins to teeter back and forth. The arena remains the same for the most part, with the only notable difference being the chaos that ensues after the sky station begins to fall apart.

NOTE

There are no Health Triggered Events during the second and third rounds of battle.

# The Tranquility

Having acquired the task of escorting a prisoner, the mighty Venator Class Jedi Cruiser "Tranquility" comes under attack by the Separatist army.

# First Round

Unlike other arenas, the Tranquility's circular, equipment-heavy bridge is an uncommon place for dueling. Add to that the constant threat of enemy fire from the surrounding hallways and you've got one of the best arenas for unconventional fighters. The console at the arena's center creates a small obstacle, while the various explosive charges make combat risky near the edges. This arena is perfect for the duelist who is good at a little of everything. You'll need all tools at your disposal to survive here.

HEALTH TRIGGERED EVENT

Once either player gets reduced to 95 percent health, the surrounding doors explode, revealing a heated battle between clone troopers and super battle droids in the background. At 70 percent health, detonators on the ground start to explode, one after another. If a Jedi player is reduced to 80 percent health and is fighting a Sith or Sith minion, the super battle droids in the left corridor start firing into the bridge.

If any Jedi player is reduced to 75 percent health and is fighting a Sith or Sith minion, the super battle droids in the right corridor start firing into the player space. If any Jedi player is reduced to 15 percent health, explosions occur in the central corridor. Clone troopers perish and battle droids run in.

# Second and Third Rounds

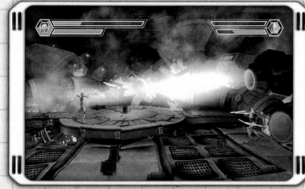

After the first round, the battle moves to the Tranquility's engine room. There, the ship is on the brink of ruin with twisted metal that's red-hot from the heat of booster fire and uncontrollable flames. The little debris that trickles into the level appears once either combatant loses 5 percent health. By far the most dangerous environmental hazards are the boosters that periodically ignite after the control panels near the arena's center (one in the foreground, one on the raised platform in the background) have been destroyed.

### HEALTH TRIGGERED EVENT

Once either player gets reduced to 95 percent health, debris begins falling in the background.

# The Negotiator

A mighty fleet of Venator-class Star Destroyers race to the Republic medical station to head off an attack by the Malevolence.

# First Round

The bridge of the mighty Negotiator is very similar to the Tranquility's first-round arena. It's a small, circular arena with plenty of equipment in the way. Unlike the Tranquility, however, the Negotiator's bridge has far fewer environmental hazards. Once the rear doors are open, stray blaster fire shoots into the main arena, causing moderate damage to whoever it hits. Aside from that, the arena is a great battleground for fighters skilled in combos and Force Attacks.

### HEALTH TRIGGERED EVENT

Once either fighter's health is reduced to 90 percent, the rear doors explode, revealing a firefight in the background. Super battle droid plasma bolts stray into the main bridge.

# Second and Third Rounds

The Negotiator is by far the largest and most awkwardly shaped arena. Its viewing room is a large circular arena with a large walkway running down its center. Though there is little in the way of environmental hazards, the room does have a few throwable objects. Otherwise, this large battleground is perfect for lightsaber purists.

## HEALTH TRIGGERED EVENT

The Malevolence will arrive based on which of the following events is triggered first.

If any Jedi fighter is reduced to 90 percent health, Separatist frigates come out of hyperspace and begin firing on the Republic forces. After a short time, the Malevolence will come out of hyperspace to join the fray.

If any Sith or Sith minion fighter is reduced to 90 percent health, Republic Venators come out of hyperspace and begin firing on the Separatist forces. The Malevolence soon comes out of hyperspace and joins the fray. After a short delay, a phalanx of Y-wing, accompanied by Anakin and Plo Koon's starfighters, soars past to attack the Malevolence.

If a Jedi player is reduced to 65 percent health, several vulture droids attack the bridge of Obi-Wan's Venator, cracking the glass. One of the Republic Venators explodes and drifts from view.

If any Sith or Sith minion player is reduced to 65 percent health, several torrents and vulture droids begin fighting in between the spacecraft, and one of the Separatist frigates explodes and drifts from view.

If any Jedi player is reduced to 50 percent health, several torrents and vulture droids begin fighting in between the spacecraft. The second Republic Venator will explode and sink from view. After both Venators have been destroyed, the Malevolence begins firing at the bridge of Obi-Wan's Venator, causing it to shudder with explosions and arcing electricity.

If any Sith or Sith minion player is reduced to 50 percent health, several torrents and vulture droids begin fighting in between the spacecraft. The second Separatist frigate will explode and sink from view.

# The Malevolence

The devastating Malevolence uses high-speed jet cars to transport cargo throughout the huge Separatist starship.

**NOTE**

There are no Health Triggered Events during the first round.

## First Round

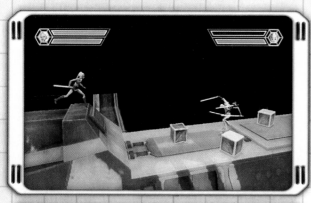

Like the Tatooine Dune Sea arena, the Malevolence arena is surprisingly complex, thanks in large part to the multicar, multitiered design. As you battle left or right along the many cars, the level changes from flat and open to cramped and multileveled. Another car, running parallel to the one you're fighting on, fires plasma bolts on you and your opponent from a distance, creating a constant environmental hazard. This makes the Malevolence the perfect arena for highly skilled combatants who can quickly switch styles.

## Second and Third Rounds

The second round of battle is much like the first. You continue the fight on the moving cars, depending on which car you ended the first round. There are no additional environmental hazards or debris.

**HEALTH TRIGGERED EVENT**

If any Sith or Sith minion player is reduced to 50 percent health, Plo Koon will appear in the background, chasing a group of vulture droids. If a Jedi player is reduced to 50 percent health, Plo Koon will appear in the background, being chased by a group of vulture droids. These events are mutually exclusive.

# Separatist Droid Lab

Deep within the secret and darkened laboratory, development nears completion on a new Separatist weapon—a droid that's capable of matching Jedi in combat.

## First Round

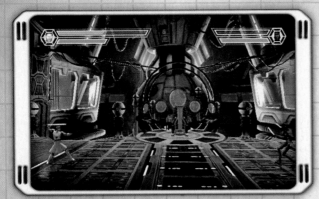

The Separatist Droid Lab is a large square arena with plenty of crates and equipment lying around for the Force Throwing duelist. However, its wide-open space and precarious edges make it a great arena for combo specialists and fighters with a penchant for knocking enemies off the arena floor. The small control niche at the battleground's top center area is a perfect place to lure an enemy and pummel him with Force Attacks.

### HEALTH TRIGGERED EVENT

Once either player gets reduced to 50 percent health, the core begins to shake as it starts overloading. Bolts of lightning arc from the core to the main arena floor.

# Second and Third Rounds

Though the location of the fight does not shift, the conditions in the arena do—severely. As the fight progresses and either combatant loses health, things get more charged. Wild bolts of electricity begin to surge throughout the entire arena. Keep a close eye on the reactors in the background so you can predict where the lightning will surge. Use this to your advantage and move your enemy into position just as the lighting unleashes!

### HEALTH TRIGGERED EVENT

Once either player gets reduced to 95 percent health, the rate of the lightning bursts increases. Once either player is reduced to 60 percent health, the core begins to go critical, tearing the whole level apart as it shakes its foundations. The rate of lightning bursts increases again.

# Sarlacc Pit

A bridge amongst the ancient ruins sits over the gaping maw of a Sarlacc within Tatooine's Dune Sea.

## First Round

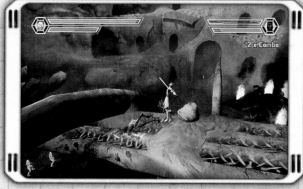

**NOTE**

There is no secondary area or Health Triggered Event.

# Mustafar

The fiery volcanic world of Mustafar.

## First Round

The fiery planet of Mustafar can be a shifty fighter's dream. The first round takes places atop a platform floating precariously over lava pits. Speedy fighters can use the wide-open circular platform to dodge enemy attacks and lure the enemy into traps as they wend around the starfighter at the platform's center. Better still, since nearly all sides of the arena are open, a clever combatant can knock the enemy off from nearly any angle. Once destroyed, the various power generators lining the arena's edges become a high-voltage system of ring ropes. Bully your enemy into a generator and watch the fun ensue as the generator explodes in a dazzling electrical display.

**NOTE**

There are no Health Triggered Events in Mustafar.

The Sarlacc Pit is a long, slender arena under constant threat of its rather large, and often unavoidable, environmental hazard. As you battle atop the long bridge, the sarlacc's tentacles whip down on the bridge, smashing you or your opponent to the floor. You can often guess which tentacle will slam down based on the tentacles' movements. If it begins to sway back and forth rapidly, move out of the way! This arena is also great for knocking enemies off the bridge and setting up combos. You can also pin enemies to either end of the bridge and overwhelm them with a barrage of blows!

who make great use of Force Energy attacks like Force Throw might struggle a bit to stay on their feet.

There are no Health Triggered Events or a secondary area for Raxus Prime.

# Second and Third Rounds

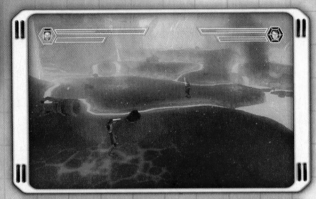

The final rounds of battle on Mustafar take place on the planet's molten surface. The multileveled arena is wide open with a small lava pit near the far right. There aren't many pieces of debris, ledges, or any environmental hazards, so this is the perfect arena for lightsaber purists.

# Raxus Prime

**The toxic, waste-covered planet of Raxus Prime.**

## First Round

The large circular arena is, like the second level of Mustafar, a lightsaber purist's playground. With little debris and no environmental hazards, the arena lends itself well to combo specialists and even shifty fighters with good agility. Bully-style fighters will have fun knocking enemies off the large platform, while combatants

# Separatist Droid Factory

**A Separatist droid manufacturing complex.**

## First Round

The T-shaped arena of the droid factory is unique. It is the only T-shaped arena, and each of its three long legs has ample room to be a small arena all on its own. The long walkway running down the center is perfect for close-quarter combat specialists who rely heavily on Smash attacks and Force attacks while the other two segments of the battle-ground are wide enough for more skilled combo fighters to develop their attacks.

There are no Health Triggered Events or a secondary area for the Separatist Droid Factory.

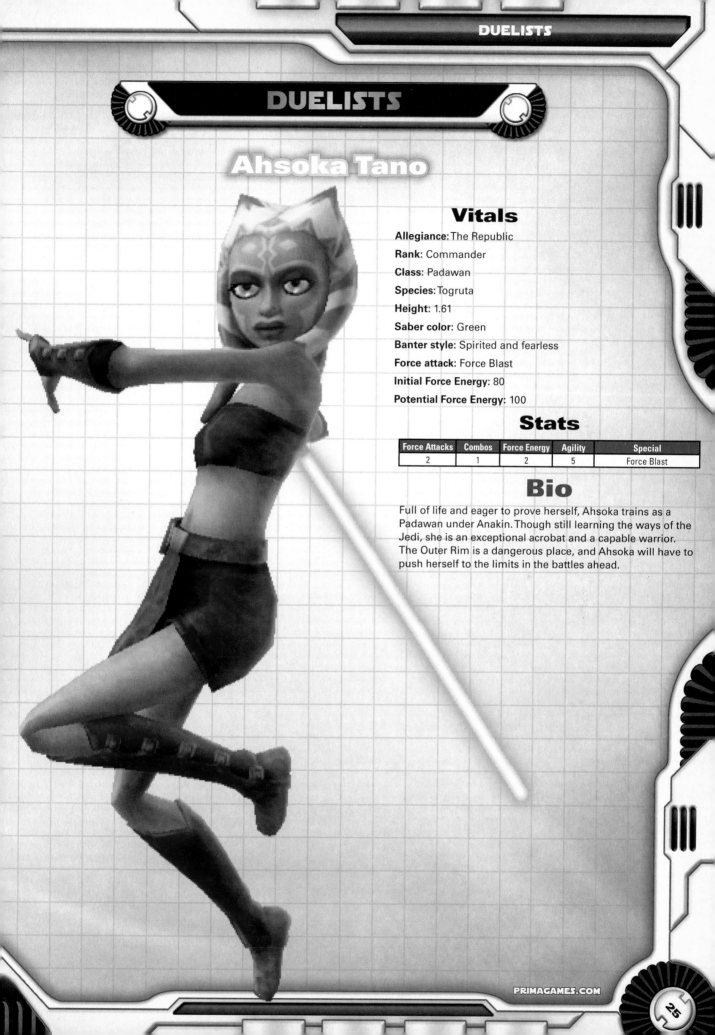

# DUELISTS

## Ahsoka Tano

### Vitals

**Allegiance:** The Republic

**Rank:** Commander

**Class:** Padawan

**Species:** Togruta

**Height:** 1.61

**Saber color:** Green

**Banter style:** Spirited and fearless

**Force attack:** Force Blast

**Initial Force Energy:** 80

**Potential Force Energy:** 100

### Stats

| Force Attacks | Combos | Force Energy | Agility | Special |
|:---:|:---:|:---:|:---:|:---:|
| 2 | 1 | 2 | 5 | Force Blast |

### Bio

Full of life and eager to prove herself, Ahsoka trains as a Padawan under Anakin. Though still learning the ways of the Jedi, she is an exceptional acrobat and a capable warrior. The Outer Rim is a dangerous place, and Ahsoka will have to push herself to the limits in the battles ahead.

# Alternate Costumes

**Standard**

**Alternate**

**Ilum Battle Gear**

**Training Outfit**

**Padawan Robes**

 **NOTE**

The costumes for all duelists are purely cosmetic.

# Fighting Style

The young Togruta Padawan uses athletic and energetic attacks to compensate for her lack of strength. She uses her Jedi training and her Togruta heritage as a basis for her attacks.

## Combos

| Signature Move | Difficulty | 1st Hit | 2nd Hit | 3rd Hit | 4th Hit | Shares Combo with... |
|---|---|---|---|---|---|---|
| Shii-Cho Slash | Easy | L | R | L | D | N/A |
| Strength of the Sarlacc | Easy | L | U | D | U | N/A |
| Rise of Virtue | Easy | R | L | R | D | Obi-Wan |
| Determined Assault | Medium | U | R | D | U | Anakin |
| Sun Djem Strike | Easy | D | U | D | — | N/A |

# Challenge Mode

## Challenge 1

| Requirement | Opponent | Level | Objective |
| --- | --- | --- | --- |
| Padawan Difficulty | Anakin Skywalker | The Resolute | Defeat the opponent in 3 minutes |

### CHALLENGER'S MOTIVATION

Anakin and Ahsoka have a young father/teenage daughter relationship, full of unspoken affection, minor frustrations, and miscommunication. But underneath it all is genuine warmth and mutual admiration. Their banter is lighthearted, with flashes of sincerity. Ahsoka is eager to prove that she is capable of being Anakin's Padawan. She does not want to appear too young or unable to be his apprentice.

This challenge can be easily accomplished as long as you keep your three-minute time limit in mind. This may seem like a long time to win a battle, but when you consider that you must win both matches within the time limit, three minutes doesn't seem long enough. Fortunately, Ahsoka is agile and speedy, making her the perfect duelist for just this type of challenge.

With one and a half minutes for each round, you've got plenty of time to string together strong combos and signature attacks against your master. Use your environment to your advantage. Hurl crates and other objects at Anakin between combos, and use stabbing attacks to break through his defense to launch even more attack strings.

## Challenge 2

| Requirement | Opponent | Level | Objective |
| --- | --- | --- | --- |
| Padawan Difficulty | Plo Koon | The Resolute | Defeat the opponent and use a Charged Combo |

### CHALLENGER'S MOTIVATION

Ahsoka considers Plo Koon to be one of her oldest friends. He is the one who first brought her to the Jedi Temple, where she felt she truly belonged. She has a deep fondness for him. Plo Koon discovered Ahsoka on her homeworld of Shili when she was a small child, and he brought her to the Jedi Temple for training. In this challenge, Ahsoka wants to prove herself to her beloved friend.

The Resolute has a lot of scattered debris and crates. Use them as projectiles against Plo Koon, and use a series of combos, parrying, and thrown objects to fill your Force Combo Gauge during the first match. When you fill the gauge, unleash a Charged Combo on your opponent, then begin refilling it again.

You don't have to finish Plo Koon with a Charged Combo; as long as you win the duel and execute a Charged Combo in either round, the challenge will be successful. However, if you execute a Charged Combo and completely miss, you'll fail, so fill your gauge several times and execute Charged Combos as many times as you can.

# Challenge 3

| Requirement | Opponent | Level | Objective |
|---|---|---|---|
| Padawan Difficulty | Obi-Wan Kenobi | The Resolute | Defeat the opponent and use at least one combo |

### CHALLENGER'S MOTIVATION

Though she respects Obi-Wan as a high-ranking Jedi officer, Ahsoka feels that his use of patience over action prevents accomplishing goals for the greater good of battle. This challenge is a perfect chance to prove to him that patience is not always a virtue.

Of all Ahsoka's challenges, this is the most manageable. Because there are no time limits, there is no pressure to finish quickly. Simply face Obi-Wan in battle and fight a smart fight. Keep your guard up and use parries to set up your combos. All you need is one; as long as you execute it during either match of the duel (and win), the challenge will be successful.

# Challenge 4

| Requirement | Opponent | Level | Objective |
|---|---|---|---|
| Jedi Knight Difficulty | Asajj Ventress | Teth Castle Dungeon | Defeat the opponent |

### CHALLENGER'S MOTIVATION

Since they first met and battled on Teth, Ahsoka has looked forward to someday facing Ventress again and putting an end to her. They have a strong hatred of each other, fueled in part by their respective rivalries with Anakin. Ahsoka is eager to prove herself by defeating the "hairless harpy."

By far, Ahsoka's most difficult challenge is facing Ventress on Jedi Knight difficulty. The shifty Ventress is speedy, dual-wields, and can be extremely aggressive. Ventress can often match your speed and launch powerful dual 'saber attacks. Exar Kun's Assault is one of her most dangerous attacks, so keep a safe distance and pick her apart with short combos.

After whittling down her health to about half, increase your attacks. Stay in close and string together combos, charged attacks, and leaping strikes. Keep your guard up whenever you're not engaged in combat, and parry occasionally. Ventress will use every power at her disposal, so stay on the move to dodge thrown objects, and watch out for her leaping attacks. If she leaps over you, either dash away or catch her as she lands behind you.

# Battle Mode

## Versus Plo Koon

**Battle Arena:** Raxus Prime

The battle against Plo Koon takes place in a wide-open arena. Take advantage of the ample space. Koon can be cagey and very hard to corner. Stalk the Jedi Master around the arena with your 'saber raised, and parry his blows. Counterattack often and always follow up with combination attacks. Use your speed to match, and eventually overwhelm him.

## Versus EG-05 Jedi Hunter

**Battle Arena:** Sarlacc Pit

The fight against the Jedi hunter droid can be one of Ahsoka's most difficult battles. You face a difficult opponent, and you must contend with the Sarlacc's tentacles slamming against the battle arena. If they slam down on you, you'll be knocked off your feet and take some damage. Stay on the move and pin the droid against the arena's far edges. Pummel it with combos and charged combo attacks to dish out the

most damage. Whenever it charges its blaster, either dash away to dodge the blast or strike it with a stabbing attack to disrupt the droid's charge.

## Versus Count Dooku

**Battle Arena:** Mustafar

Dooku is a patient fighter. He won't try to overwhelm you with a flurry of attacks, and he won't execute a lot of leaping attacks to try and throw you off guard. Instead, he'll wait for you to attack and then counter with devastating efficiency. If you try picking him apart, he'll block, parry, or counterattack until you're done. However, if you attack and keep constant pressure on him, he'll be unable to constantly defend.

Force Count Dooku to go where you want him to go and bully him into environmental hazards. During the second match, use the multitiered level to gain an advantage. Hop onto raised areas, luring Dooku toward you, then ambush him from higher ground as he approaches.

# Versus General Grievous

**Battle Arena:** Droid Factory

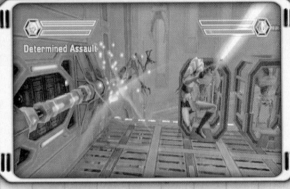

General Grievous can be a tough fight. His multi-lightsaber attack can be very difficult to parry or even defend. Stay on the move and use your speed to attack Grievous from all sides. Pummel Grievous from one side, then quickly shift to his other and attack. Keep the general on his metal toes and rivets. Steer clear of his Saber Storm attack by either rolling away or leaping over it. Corner Grievous against the arena's edge, spin him around with a Force-imbued attack, then follow up with signature moves like Sun Djem Strike.

# Versus Ahsoka Tano

**Battle Arena:** The Resolute

Facing yourself in battle is both a blessing and a curse. You know what you're capable of, so you shouldn't be surprised. Unfortunately, you have to deal with someone who is as agile and fast as you. Anticipate Ahsoka's attacks and parry her initial blows. Don't let her start any combo strings or you'll be in a heap of trouble. Parry attacks and counter with your own combos to keep your doppleganger on the defensive.

# Versus Asajj Ventress

**Battle Arena:** The Malevolence

Ventress is fast, furious, and very powerful. Refrain from standing toe-to-toe with the bald baddy and instead make her chase you. Dodge her powerful signature attacks like Exar Kun's Assault and Dark Acolyte Strike, then swing around to her rear and counter. As she approaches, use Force Combos to knock her away and spin her around. Use the arena's multiple areas to your advantage by making Ventress navigate over barriers and across gaps. When she does, ambush her with strong combo strings.

# Anakin Skywalker

## Vitals

**Allegiance:** The Republic

**Rank:** General

**Class:** Jedi Knight

**Species:** Human

**Height:** 1.88

**Saber color:** Blue

**Banter style:** Confident and determined

**Force attack:** Force Blast

**Initial Force Energy:** 100

**Potential Force Energy:** 125

## Stats

| Force Attacks | Combos | Force Energy | Agility | Special |
|---|---|---|---|---|
| 2 | 5 | 4 | 3 | Force Blast |

## Bio

As an accomplished Jedi and commander in the Grand Army of the Republic, Anakin has developed into a formidable warrior and tactician. Since the events at the Battle of Christophsis, he now shoulders the responsibility of mentoring a new Padawan, Ahsoka Tano. Learning to balance his mission priorities with his desire to guide and protect Ahsoka will create some difficult challenges that Anakin must overcome.

## Alternate Costumes

**Standard**

**Alternate**

**ARC Battle Gear**

**Tatooine Battle Gear**

**Jedi Knight Robes**

# Fighting Style

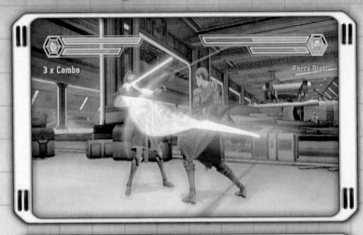

Anakin is a powerful Jedi Knight with great lightsaber skills. He is one of the few duelists who can combine exceptional 'saber skills with strong Force Power attacks.

## Combos

| Signature Move | Difficulty | 1st Hit | 2nd Hit | 3rd Hit | 4th Hit | Shares Combo with... |
|---|---|---|---|---|---|---|
| Tail of the Dragon | Easy | L | R | U | — | N/A |
| Jung Ma Assault | Easy | R | L | D | — | N/A |
| Dune Sea Storm | Medium | L | U | R | — | N/A |
| Focused Offense | Medium | U | R | D | U | Ahsoka Tano |
| Determined Assault | Hard | R | D | L | U | Obi-Wan Kenobi |

# Challenge Mode

## Challenge 1

| Requirement | Opponent | Level | Objective |
|---|---|---|---|
| Padawan Difficulty | Obi-Wan Kenobi | The Resolute | Defeat the opponent without using the Force. |

### CHALLENGER'S MOTIVATION

Their challenge is one of playful camaraderie, like brothers competing with each other—there is genuine warmth and respect underneath. Sometimes Anakin's pride shines through, however. He feels a special attachment to Obi-Wan, who was like the father he never had. Master and apprentice have formed a special bond throughout Anakin's adolescence. In Anakin's own words, "Obi-Wan is a great mentor, as wise as Master Yoda, and as powerful as Master Windu; I am truly thankful to be his apprentice." But make no mistake about it—Anakin intends on winning this challenge.

Obi-Wan Kenobi is a skilled lightsaber duelist but is surprisingly susceptible to long strings of combos and signature attacks. Use a combination of leaping attacks to get around his defense and attack from behind. After dropping him with a leaping slash, catch the grizzled Jedi with a combination attack as he gets back to his feet.

After delivering at least one combo attack, back off a bit and employ a defensive posture. Keep your lightsaber up and ready to parry, then pick away at your former master until you defeat him and win the challenge.

### CAUTION

If you use a Charged Combo, Force-imbued attacks, special attacks, or Force Throw, you'll fail the challenge.

## Challenge 2

| Requirement | Opponent | Level | Objective |
|---|---|---|---|
| Padawan Difficulty | Asajj Ventress | Teth Castle Dungeon | Defeat the opponent and use one parry and win a Lightsaber Lock. |

### CHALLENGER'S MOTIVATION

During his first fight with Ventress, Anakin repeatedly strikes her with her own lightsaber. During this attack, he had disturbing visions and was deeply troubled by what he had done. Anakin knew his win only came from tapping into his dark side. Ventress is also responsible for the scar over Anakin's eye.

  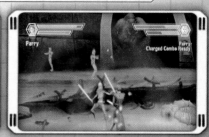

Ventress is a very dangerous duelist. She's fast and relentless with her dual lightsabers. Keep your guard up and deflect her combo attacks. After successfully defending Ventress's strongest attacks, like Exar Kun's Assault and Dark Acolyte Strike, parry at least one noncombo attack. Ventress's combos are too complicated to parry consistently, so focus instead on parrying her simpler attacks.

After parrying at least one blow, increase the intensity of your attacks. You can't choose when to engage in a Lightsaber Lock, but by increasing your rate of attack, you'll increase the chances of engaging in a lock. Win the Lightsaber Lock, then finish the fight as you would in any other mode, with combos, Force-imbued attacks, and strong defense.

# Challenge 3

| Requirement | Opponent | Level | Objective |
|---|---|---|---|
| Padawan Difficulty | Mace Windu | Droid Factory | Defeat the opponent and use at least one combo. |

### CHALLENGER'S MOTIVATION

Anakin has respect for Mace Windu, as he is an extremely talented Jedi. However, he does not completely feel that Mace believes in him or his ability as a Jedi. Anakin and Mace have a somewhat chilly relationship. Windu disapproved of his training from the beginning, due to Anakin's age and his preexisting attachments, but his obvious power and the prophecy made him relent. Mace is impressed by Skywalker's skills and dedication, yet remains wary of his susceptibility to falling toward the dark side. For his part, Anakin wants to prove himself to this stern father figure.

Master Mace Windu is one of the most difficult combatants you will face. He's very strong physically, he's fast, and he's very gifted in the ways of the Force. Add to that a strong mastery of a unique lightsaber form and you've got one of the most powerful Jedi ever.

The only way to best Windu is to capitalize on all Lightsaber Locks and to match the Jedi Master's intensity. If you are consistently in a defensive posture, Mace Windu will break through your defense every time and slice off huge chunks of health. Instead, parry his attacks and follow with combos like Jung Ma Assault. Overwhelm Windu with your combos and put an end to the Jedi Master.

# Challenge 4

| Requirement | Opponent | Level | Objective |
|---|---|---|---|
| Jedi Knight Difficulty | Anakin Skywalker | Tatooine Dune Sea | Defeat the opponent. |

### CHALLENGER'S MOTIVATION

War has molded Anakin into a man and has honed his combat ability, but it continues to nourish his ego. Anakin is quite boastful and cocky and is likely to remain that way against himself.

The battle against your doppleganger is a fun one. You've no restrictions other than to not lose, so approach this battle as you would against Obi-Wan Kenobi or Count Dooku. Mix up your attacks, split up your signature combos with smaller two-hit or three-hit combos, and parry as much as possible.

Use the environment to your advantage by hurling objects at your twin and make short work of the imposter.

# Battle Mode

## Versus Obi-Wan Kenobi

**Battle Arena:** Raxus Prime

Obi-Wan Kenobi is a formidable opponent no matter what arena you're in. Though Obi-Wan is susceptible to combo attacks, the wide-open Raxus Prime arena make it difficult to pin him down and pummel him with long combos. Follow the Jedi Master around the arena, slowly picking away at him with short combos until he's below 50 percent health. Once he is at 50 percent, use Force-imbued attacks to break his defenses and follow it up with signature attacks.

## Versus Count Dooku

**Battle Arena:** Sarlacc Pit

Dooku is the most defensive duelist in the game. He'll block nearly every attack if you try to pick away at him. Instead, attack the Count with lots of attacks that are designed to break through tough defense like Force-imbued attacks, leaping slashes, and stabbing attacks. Once you've disrupted Dooku's defense, dish out more damage with devastating combos. Stay on the move to avoid the Sarlacc's tentacles.

## Versus Kit Fisto

**Battle Arena:** Mustafar

Kit Fisto is a dangerous opponent. He's agile and highly skilled with the lightsaber. Parry Fisto's attacks consistently to keep him from launching long combos and force him into the electrical currents surging around the arena. Once in the secondary area of the arena, use the uneven ground to your advantage. Lure Fisto around the arena and ambush him with leaping attacks as he approaches.

# Versus Mace Windu

**Battle Arena:** Droid Factory

Mace Windu will finish you off quickly if he gets on a roll. Keep him from doing so by fighting his kind of fight—fast, furious, and full of combos. Don't let up on the Jedi Knight. Use attacks like Tail of the Dragon and charged combos to dish out the most damage. Vary your attacks to keep him off guard and capitalize after he's missed with his Force Blast attacks, which is when he is most vulnerable.

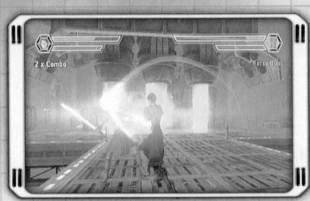

# Versus Anakin Skywalker

**Battle Arena:** The Resolute

Fighting against yourself can be tricky. Your "clone" will keep a stout guard and try to parry often. String together your attacks with short two- and three-hit combos and break through your twin's defense with leaping and stabbing attacks.

# Versus EG-05 Jedi Hunter

**Battle Arena:** The Malevolence

Fighting the EG-05 Jedi hunter is a lot like facing Asajj Ventress. Since both share a talent for dual lightsabers, they can both be difficult to defend against. Stay on the move to keep from getting fried by the rogue electrical currents, and use your speed to get around the killer droid. Attack it from all angles, avoiding its strikes as you move, and pummel the pile of junk parts with plenty of Force attacks.

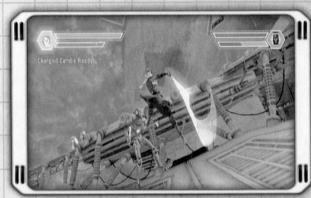

# Asajj Ventress

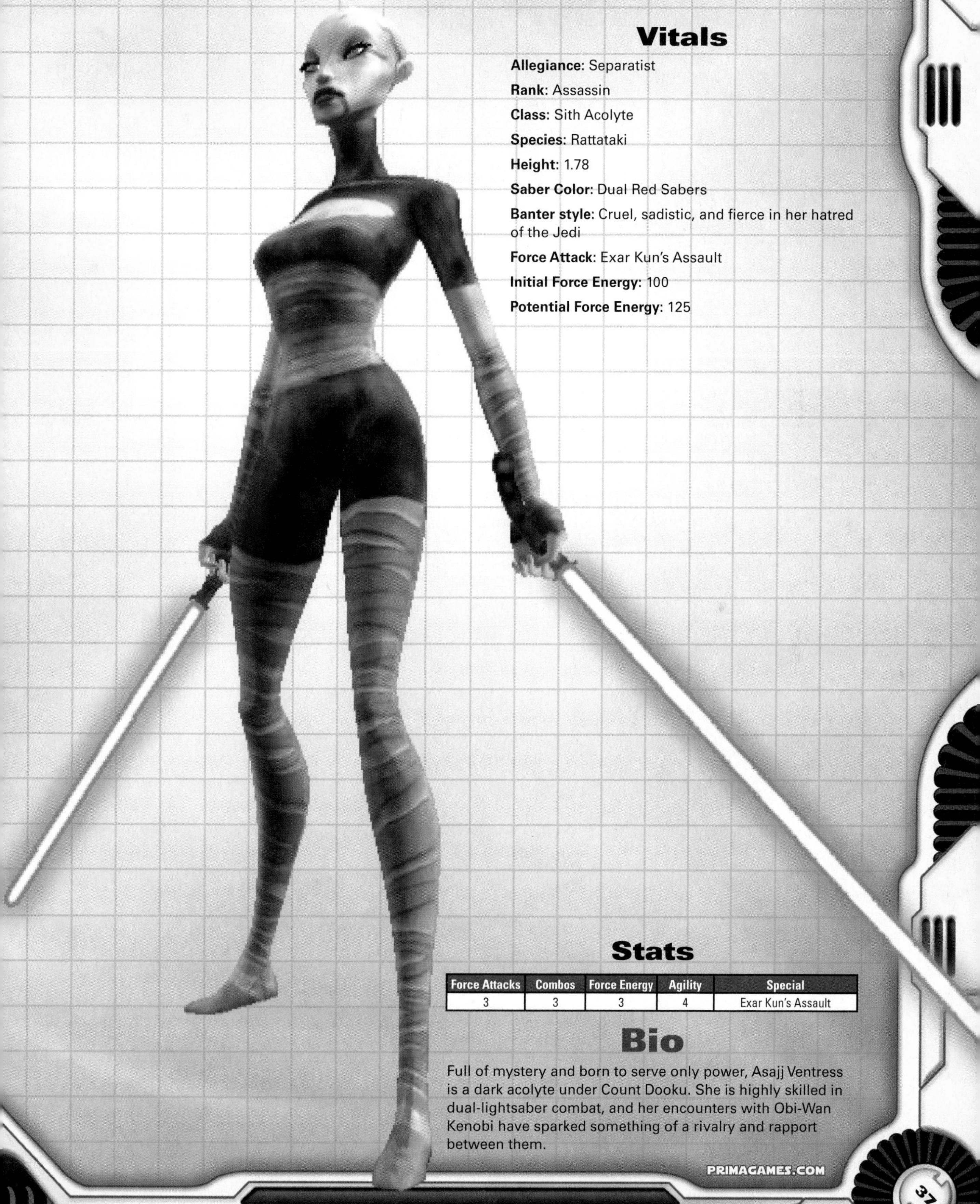

## Vitals

**Allegiance:** Separatist

**Rank:** Assassin

**Class:** Sith Acolyte

**Species:** Rattataki

**Height:** 1.78

**Saber Color:** Dual Red Sabers

**Banter style:** Cruel, sadistic, and fierce in her hatred of the Jedi

**Force Attack:** Exar Kun's Assault

**Initial Force Energy:** 100

**Potential Force Energy:** 125

## Stats

| Force Attacks | Combos | Force Energy | Agility | Special |
|---|---|---|---|---|
| 3 | 3 | 3 | 4 | Exar Kun's Assault |

## Bio

Full of mystery and born to serve only power, Asajj Ventress is a dark acolyte under Count Dooku. She is highly skilled in dual-lightsaber combat, and her encounters with Obi-Wan Kenobi have sparked something of a rivalry and rapport between them.

# LIGHTSABER DUELS

## Alternate Costumes

**Standard**

**Alternate**

**Gladiatorial Outfit**

**Assassin Battle Gear**

**Acolyte Robes**

## Fighting Style

PRIMA OFFICIAL GAME GUIDE

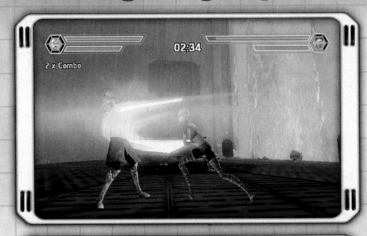

Asajj Ventress is a skilled combatant with the lightsaber. Unfortunately for her opponent, she's able to wield two 'sabers in combat. In combination with her high Agility rating, Ventress can execute several strong combos and devastating dual-lightsaber attacks.

## Combos

| Signature Move | Difficulty | 1st Hit | 2nd Hit | 3rd Hit | 4th Hit | Shares Combo with... |
| Saber Storm | Easy | L | R | L | — | EG-05 Jedi hunter droid |
| Rage of the Rancor | Easy | R | L | U | — | N/A |
| Dark Acolyte Strike | Easy | U | D | U | D | N/A |
| Path of Suffering | Medium | D | L | R | D | N/A |
| Wrath of Hatred | Hard | R | D | L | U | N/A |

# Challenge Mode

## Challenge 1

| Requirement | Opponent | Level | Objective |
| --- | --- | --- | --- |
| Jedi Knight Difficulty | Obi-Wan Kenobi | Mustafar | Defeat the opponent within three minutes. |

### CHALLENGER'S MOTIVATION

Obi-Wan was once believed dead after being captured by Asajj Ventress. While he was in captivity, Ventress used a Sith torture mask that obscured his connection to the Force. She did that to show Obi-Wan's uselessness to Count Dooku.

Defeating a Jedi within three minutes at Jedi Knight difficulty is no small task, even for the mighty Asajj Ventress. To win this challenge, allot one and half minutes per round and turn up the heat on your plan of attack. Obi-Wan is a defensive fighter but can be quickly overtaken with a flurry of combos and strong attacks. Break through his defense, then attack with Saber Storm and Rage of the Rancor combos.

If he attempts to circle around behind you, block his blow, then counter with Exar Kun's Assault. As long as you keep constant pressure on the bearded Jedi general, he'll succumb to your speed and superior fight plan.

## Challenge 2

| Requirement | Opponent | Level | Objective |
| --- | --- | --- | --- |
| Jedi Knight Difficulty | Kit Fisto | The Resolute | Defeat the opponent within three minutes. |

### CHALLENGER'S MOTIVATION

Kit Fisto and Ventress once battled to the brink of death. Ventress hates Jedi and has made it her duty to rid the galaxy of Jedi in order to gain Count Dooku's praises.

Kit Fisto is another formidable Jedi opponent. Unlike his colleague Obi-Wan, Fisto is a bit more fiery when it comes to lightsaber battle. What Obi-Wan has in patience, Fisto has in confidence. Left unchecked, Kit Fisto could easily dismantle you by chipping away small bits of health with short combos and in-and-out attacks. Block his advances and turn his confidence on him.

Attack the tentacled Jedi with short combos, stabbing attacks, and a healthy dose of Exar Kun's Assaults. If he attempts to back away and retreat, use the surrounding debris to slow him down and create more openings for combos.

# Challenge 3

| Requirement | Opponent | Level | Objective |
|---|---|---|---|
| Jedi Knight Difficulty | Mace Windu | Raxus Prime | Defeat the opponent within three minutes. |

## CHALLENGER'S MOTIVATION

While on a mission as an assassin, Ventress tricked some people into believing Windu had hired her in order to accomplish her task. When the truth was eventually uncovered, Ventress briefly dueled Mace Windu before she realized she was no match for his skill.

Of the four challengers, Mace Windu may be the most difficult. His unique combination of power, speed, and an aggressive fighting technique make him one of the most formidable Jedi to grace the Council halls. In order to win—and survive—the encounter with Windu, you must block and parry nearly every chance you get. Windu won't often let up on his attack, so chances to parry and counterattack should be plentiful.

Counterattack as often as possible and mix in plenty of short two- and three-hit combos to keep things fresh. If he gets out of range, don't chase him; he'll probably come back to you immediately. When he does, greet him with Force attacks and Dark Acolyte Strikes.

# Challenge 4

| Requirement | Opponent | Level | Objective |
|---|---|---|---|
| Jedi Knight Difficulty | Plo Koon | Droid Factory | Defeat the opponent within three minutes. |

## CHALLENGER'S MOTIVATION

Even though Koon knows that Ventress is nothing more than Count Dooku's assassin, he also knows not to underestimate her desire to be one with the dark side. Ventress's deep hatred for all Jedi fuels her desire to defeat Koon in battle.

As quick as Koon is, he can be a very defensive fighter, often slowing him down to his detriment. Use the Droid Factory's tight walkways to your advantage by unleashing a constant stream of combos on Koon and cornering him against the arena's edges. If he blocks, use stabbing attacks to break his defense and follow it with Wrath of Hatred attacks.

Koon is very capable of stringing together long chains of two- and three-hit combos, so don't let your guard down in your zeal to pummel him. Instead, keep a steady pressure on him, but block between hits. Once you've got him cornered, unleash Exar Kun's Assault to slice him up, then skewer him into little Koon kabobs.

# Battle Mode

## Versus Count Dooku

**Battle Arena:** Raxus Prime

The battle against your master can be a quick one. Dooku waits for just the right moment to strike. He'll carefully block your attacks until you give him an opening, and then he'll pounce. Don't give him the chance to do so! Rush into Dooku's defense with a stab attack, then hit him with a combo before retreating and doing it again. If you are constantly on the offensive, he'll find an opening, exploit it, and slice off nearly half your health before you realize what happened.

## Versus Mace Windu

**Battle Arena:** Sarlacc Pit

Aside from Count Dooku, Mace Windu may be your most difficult fight in Battle mode. Stay light on your feet and constantly dodge the Sarlacc tentacles. Bully Windu to the bridge's edge, and pin him with a flood of 'saber strikes. Drive him back with Exar Kun's Assault, then use leaping attacks to get to his rear. If you watch the tentacles closely, you can even bully Windu into their path to deal extra damage!

## Versus Ahsoka Tano

**Battle Arena:** Mustafar

Ahsoka Tano is the fastest fighter in the game. When the battle begins, put on the heat and don't let up. Take control of the fight with signature attacks and short combos to keep Tano on the defensive. If she takes control of the fight, she'll zip around you and pester you with quick 'saber strikes. Swat the speedy Ahsoka and turn the tables on her with leaping lightsaber slashes and Force Throw attacks.

## Versus Plo Koon

**Battle Arena:** Droid Factory

Like Ahsoka, Koon can whittle away at you with lots of short combos. Make short work of the masked Jedi by cornering him against the arena's edge and pummeling him with lots of combos. Knock Koon back with Rage of the Rancor, then follow it up with other combos like Saber Storm and Dark Acolyte Strike. This fight is very similar to Ventress's Plo Koon challenge. Once cornered, cut Koon with Exar Kun's Assault. Koon's attacks can be parried easily, since he tends to be a bit more defensive. Use this to charge your Force Gauge and unleash Force combos on the Jedi Knight.

## Versus Asajj Ventress

**Battle Arena:** The Malevolence

Surprisingly, the battle against yourself isn't as challenging as you might expect. You can match your opponent speed for speed, so keeping up with your mirror self shouldn't be difficult. This match is decided by which fighter can get out ahead first. As soon as the fight begins, hurl one of the crates on the tram at your opponent and throw her off balance; then rush at her and execute Path of Suffering to inflict moderate damage. Follow Ventress around the arena as she tries to leap and roll away from your attack, but keep a steady stream of 'saber strikes swinging as you go. Eventually, it'll be clear which is the better "bald witch"—you.

## Versus Anakin Skywalker

**Battle Arena:** Teth Castle Dungeon

The best approach for this battle is to keep a balanced technique. Don't stay on the offensive too long, but don't block for too long either. Parry Anakin's attacks, follow with a combo, then retreat to a defensive posture to guard against his retaliation. Even after you take control of the fight, Anakin can still overwhelm you with combos and surprise you in the end. If you underestimate him or count him out before the fight is won, you'll surely pay for it.

# Count Dooku

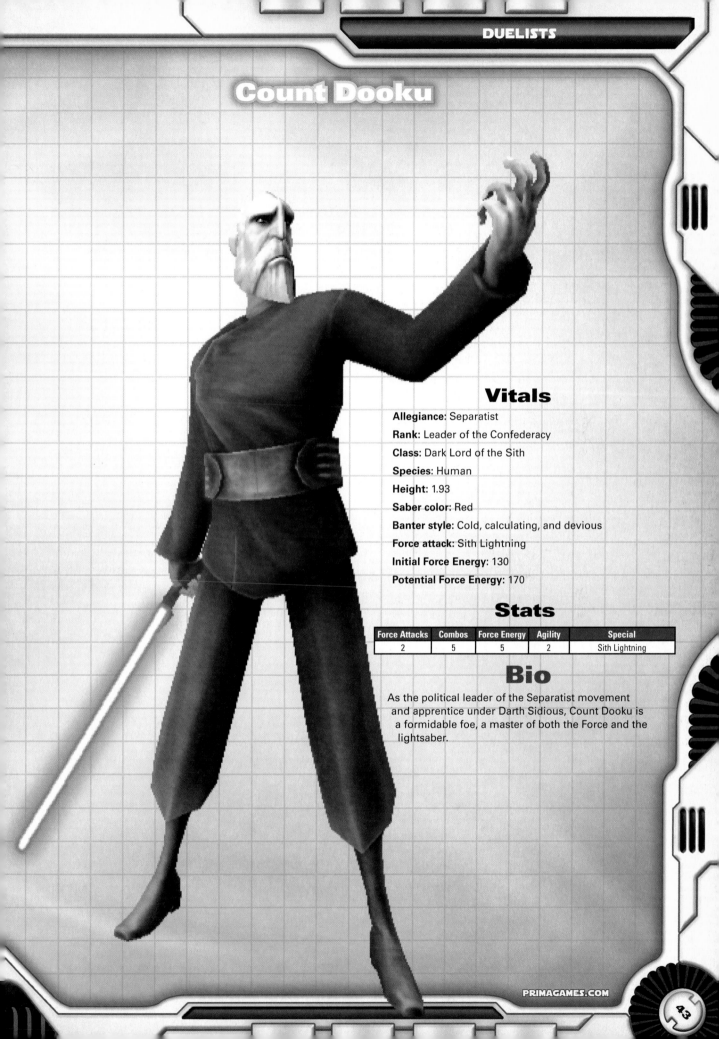

## Vitals

**Allegiance:** Separatist

**Rank:** Leader of the Confederacy

**Class:** Dark Lord of the Sith

**Species:** Human

**Height:** 1.93

**Saber color:** Red

**Banter style:** Cold, calculating, and devious

**Force attack:** Sith Lightning

**Initial Force Energy:** 130

**Potential Force Energy:** 170

## Stats

| Force Attacks | Combos | Force Energy | Agility | Special |
|---|---|---|---|---|
| 2 | 5 | 5 | 2 | Sith Lightning |

## Bio

As the political leader of the Separatist movement and apprentice under Darth Sidious, Count Dooku is a formidable foe, a master of both the Force and the lightsaber.

# Alternate Costumes

**Standard**

**Alternate**

**Separatist Uniform**

**Confederacy Battle Gear**

**Sith Robes**

# Fighting Style

Count Dooku's fighting style can best be described as regal. He's controlled, calm, and calculating. Rather than use his Force abilities, he utilizes attacks designed specifically for lightsaber combat.

## Combos

| Signature Move | Difficulty | 1st Hit | 2nd Hit | 3rd Hit | 4th Hit | Shares Combo with... |
|---|---|---|---|---|---|---|
| Makeshi Retort | Easy | L | R | S | — | N/A |
| Ensnaring Surge | Easy | R | L | D | — | N/A |
| Superior Deception | Medium | D | R | U | D | N/A |
| Tyranus's Deception | Medium | D | L | R | U | N/A |
| Shroud of the Dark Side | Hard | L | D | L | U | N/A |

# Challenge Mode

## Challenge 1

| Requirement | Opponent | Level | Objective |
|---|---|---|---|
| Jedi Knight Difficulty | Asajj Ventress | Raxus Prime | Defeat the opponent and use all five combos and at least one Charged Combo |

### CHALLENGER'S MOTIVATION

Knowing Ventress's assignment was one of Darth Sidious's double-edged schemes, her success in killing Anakin Skywalker would mean Asajj was a better replacement for Count Dooku than Skywalker, making her as much of a threat as she is an ally. Dooku sees Ventress as a tool, a talented emissary he can send to enforce his will. He can't acknowledge her as a true Sith apprentice without alarming his own master, Darth Sidious, but that doesn't prevent him from manipulating her ambitions for his own ends.

 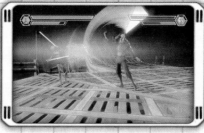 

Battling Asajj Ventress can be difficult, especially in the wide-open arena of Raxus Prime. There, the vile vixen Ventress can leap, dash, and roll freely around the arena as she dodges your attacks. Be patient during the battle, as there is no time limit, but don't let Ventress get too far. You need her to be close enough so that, at the very least, the final hit of your combos makes contact with her.

To connect cleanly with all five combos, wait for her to execute Exar Kun's Assault, then dodge out of the way. After she misses, she'll be temporarily winded, granting you a perfect opportunity to land a combo. Start with your hardest combo, Shroud of the Dark Side, and work your way down to the easiest. By the time you've connected with all five combos, your Force Gauge should be ready to unleash a Charged Combo.

### TIP

No rule states that you must meet all the challenge requirements within two rounds. If you execute four of the five combos and your opponent is close to defeat for the second time, you can throw one round (intentionally take a loss) and get a completely fresh Health bar to execute the final combo or meet the final requirement.

## Challenge 2

| Requirement | Opponent | Level | Objective |
|---|---|---|---|
| Jedi Knight Difficulty | General Grievous | Raxus Prime | Defeat the opponent; use all five combos and knock him out of the level. |

### CHALLENGER'S MOTIVATION

Knowing he would never willingly join Count Dooku after nearly killing him, Dooku encased what was left of Grievous in a metal body and rebuilt him. The resulting creation retained only part of the brain, the eyes, and a sack of organs. The general's brain was altered to make him a perfect tool and, with Dooku's training, a deadly killer of Jedi. Dooku trained Grievous in lightsaber combat and made him the general of the droid army. This challenge emulates one of their many training sessions.

This challenge is not much different from the previous one. Instead of using a Charged Combo, however, you must knock Grievous off the arena at least once. As long as you're not fighting squarely at the arena's center, you could kill two birds with one stone. Begin by hitting Grievous with Makeshi Retort and Ensnaring Surge. With the two shortest combos performed, you can maneuver the general toward the arena's edge and use any of the remaining three combos to knock Grievous off the platform.

If you cannot knock him off with one of the other three combos, then perform them as you would during a normal fight, then use Force Attacks like Smash Attack to knock the general off.

# Challenge 3

| Requirement | Opponent | Level | Objective |
|---|---|---|---|
| Jedi Knight Difficulty | EG-05 Jedi Hunter | Raxus Prime | Defeat the opponent, use all five combos, and parry five attacks. |

### CHALLENGER'S MOTIVATION

Dooku is skeptical that a droid will be able to reliably defeat a Jedi, but he is pleased to have another weapon in his arsenal. Before he can set the Jedi hunter loose, he must test the droid's skills.

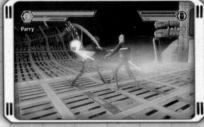

This is Dooku's most difficult challenge. The EG-05 Jedi hunter droid is incredibly fast and shifty, making it very difficult to execute combos cleanly. To make matters worse, its dual lightsabers make parrying tricky. Still, if anyone has the patience and skill to do it, Count Dooku can. Like Ventress and Grievous, the Jedi hunter droid has several attacks that leave him vulnerable if he misses. His Dark Blast, for example, leaves him open to counterattack if you sidestep the blast. Use this to execute your combos cleanly.

After you execute all the combos, spend the rest of the time parrying his attacks. Don't leave the combos for last, because he's too fast and there's no guarantee that you'll get all five before either you or he is defeated. If you're comfortable with your parrying skills, however, use them to set up your combos and give the droid a much deserved beating.

# Challenge 4

| Requirement | Opponent | Level | Objective |
|---|---|---|---|
| Jedi Knight Difficulty | Anakin Skywalker | Tatooine | Defeat the opponent in under three minutes and use all five combos. |

### CHALLENGER'S MOTIVATION

Anakin and Dooku first fought on Geonosis. Despite holding his own against Dooku, Anakin lost his hand in the end, as Dooku was the superior swordsman. The count is intrigued by Anakin, the so-called Chosen One of Jedi prophecy. He senses Anakin's power and is wary of it, even though he cut off his hand during their first confrontation.

The final challenge should be no problem if you've managed to complete the previous three. Instead of having to execute all five combos and another objective, all you must do is execute the five combos and defeat Anakin within three minutes. Begin by performing the harder Shroud of the Dark Side combo, then use Superior Deception and Tyranus's Deception. Leave the easiest two combos—Makeshi Retort and Ensnaring Surge—for last.

Use parries and Force attacks to spin Anakin around and set up your combo attacks. Keep your guard up once he's back on the offensive. You may have three rounds to execute your five combos, but you'll run out of time before you can meet the challenge. That is why speed is of the essence for this challenge.

# Battle Mode

## Versus EG-05 Jedi Hunter Droid

**Battle Arena:** Raxus Prime

The Jedi hunter droid is a lot like Asajj Ventress—fast, shifty, and totes two 'sabers. Approach this fight just as you would a fight with your pale pupil. Keep your guard up, be patient, and wait for your rival to give you an opening. Instead of Ventress's Saber Storm attack, the droid charges and fires a blast of dark energy. Either sidestep its blast or strike the bucket of bolts as it charges, then follow up with combo attacks.

## Versus Kit Fisto

**Battle Arena:** Sarlacc Pit

The small bridge of the Sarlacc Pit arena is the perfect place for close-quarter combat. Use a healthy dose of Force Lightning attacks and your shorter, speedier combos like Makeshi Retort and Ensnaring Surge to whittle down Kit Fisto. If he gets too close for comfort, use Smash attacks to knock him off the bridge and create some breathing room. Raise your 'saber to block his attack as he returns, then counter with your own combo.

PRIMA OFFICIAL GAME GUIDE

# Versus Anakin Skywalker

**Battle Arena:** Mustafar

The fastest way to win this match is to parry most of Anakin's attacks and land short two- and three-hit combos to whittle his health. Hurl nearby objects to fill up your Force Gauge, then unleash your charge combo to pummel the pedantic former Padawan. Repeat this process several times to singe huge chunks of health in no time at all.

# Versus Count Dooku

**Battle Arena:** Separatist Listening Post

As you might expect, the battle against your twin can be very difficult. Expect Dooku to block and parry frequently, making your initial attacks either backfire or glance off his 'saber harmlessly. To keep from being countered into defeat, use unconventional methods to circumvent his guard. Execute stabbing attacks, leaping slashes, and lots of sidestepping to get a better angle on your mirror self. Once you've broken through or sidestepped his defense, smash him with Force Attacks and combos.

# Versus Mace Windu

**Battle Arena:** Droid Factory

Do not take Mace Windu lightly. Little two- and three-hit combos won't be enough to chop him down. Instead, rely heavily on your signature attacks, namely Tyranus's Deception, Superior Deception, and Shroud of the Dark Side. Use these combos frequently, stopping only to parry his attacks and execute charged combos.

# Versus Obi-Wan Kenobi

**Battle Arena:** Teth Castle Ramparts

Obi-Wan is a patient fighter, just like you. Approach this battle as you would a battle against Anakin. Keep your guard up and parry his attacks. If you get too far from your opponent, be ready to sidestep projectiles and defend against his Force Blast attack. Once you're in close, stun him with Sith Lightning and follow it up with quick combos.

# EG-05 Jedi Hunter

## Vitals

**Allegiance:** Separatist

**Rank:** Assassin

**Class:** Jedi Hunter

**Species:** Droid

**Height:** 1.8

**Saber color:** Red

**Banter style:** N/A

**Force Attack:** Dark Blast

**Initial Force Energy:** N/A

**Potential Force Energy:** N/A

## Stats

| Force Attacks | Combos | Force Energy | Agility | Special |
|---|---|---|---|---|
| 2 | 5 | 5 | 2 | Sith Lightning |

## Bio

The Separatists are losing support in the Colonies; they say the battles are won because a Jedi is worth a hundred droids, so now Count Dooku has created an assassin that could turn the tide of the entire war. A new assassin designed to hunt down and eliminate the Jedi, the cold and merciless EG-05 Jedi hunter droid is completely devoid of compassion when acting out Count Dooku's orders.

## Alternate Costumes

**Standard**

**Alternate**

**EG-2 Prototype**

**EG-3 Prototype**

**EG-4 Prototype**

## Fighting Style

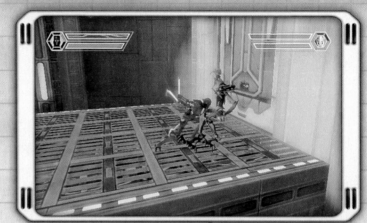

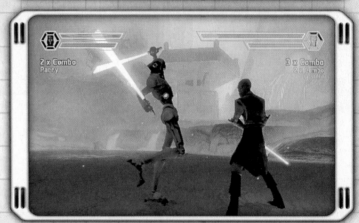

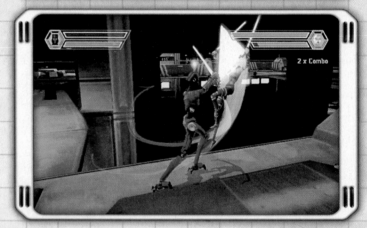

With the fighting style of Ventress, the technology of Grievous, and the markings of its Sith heritage, the EG-05 Jedi hunter droid is a unique living weapon trained by Dooku. It is always ready to execute his slightest command.

## Combos

| Signature Move | Difficulty | 1st Hit | 2nd Hit | 3rd Hit | 4th Hit | Shares Combo with... |
|---|---|---|---|---|---|---|
| Saber Storm | Easy | L | R | L | — | Asajj Ventress and General Greivous |
| Dark Execution | Easy | L | U | D | U | N/A |
| Separatist's Fury | Easy | R | L | R | U | N/A |
| Niman's Onslaught | Hard | U | L | D | R | N/A |
| Assassin's Sokan | Hard | D | U | L | D | N/A |

# Challenge Mode

## Challenge 1

| Requirement | Opponent | Level | Objective |
|---|---|---|---|
| Jedi Knight Difficulty | EG-1 Prototype | Droid Factory | Defeat the opponent and use at least one combo and Dark Blast. |

**NOTE**

Because the EG-05 Jedi hunter droid is programmed to follow Count Dooku's every command, he lacks the need for motivation. He does what he is told without question. Besides, he wasn't built with vocal processors.

This first challenge against a prototype droid is the easiest. Execute Saber Storm to knock your opponent away, then follow it up with a Dark Blast to fulfill the challenge requirements. Once that is done, you need only to defeat the droid two more times.

Even though there's no need to execute other combos during this fight, use this first challenge to practice harder combos like Assassin's Sokan and Niman's Onslaught. It will help you in later challenges, and it is a surefire way to keep your opponent on its back in this challenge.

## Challenge 2

| Requirement | Opponent | Level | Objective |
|---|---|---|---|
| Jedi Knight Difficulty | EG-2 Prototype | The Malevolence | Defeat the opponent. Use three combos and knock it out of the level. |

During this challenge, begin by knocking your opponent back with Dark Blast, then immediately rush it as it gets back on its feet. Once it does, slash it with Saber Storm, then Dark Execution. Corner your predecessor against the edge of the tram and pummel it with short combos, then hit it with Niman's Onslaught. As the creature is about to get up, execute a Smash attack and send it flying off the tram.

The prototype won't just stand there and let you beat it to bits, so be fast and very aggressive as soon as the fight begins. If the EG-2 manages to slash you back, retreat to a distant part of the tram and wait for it to approach you. When it does, attack it and take control of the fight.

# Challenge 3

| Requirement | Opponent | Level | Objective |
|---|---|---|---|
| Jedi Knight Difficulty | EG-3 Prototype | Separatist Listening Post | Defeat the opponent, and use all five combos and two Charged Combos. |

In order to complete this challenge, you'll need to do some precise planning. Split up the tasks you need to perform by rounds. Execute two or three combos in the first round, preferably the three hardest, and one Charged Combo. That way, you don't have to struggle to execute all five combos or both charged combos in one round. Instead, you can execute three combos in round one, fill up your Force Gauge with a few parries, then finish off your opponent with a Charged Combo.

In the second round (or third, if necessary) you can focus on executing fewer combos and concentrate on landing the second required Charged Combo. The EG-3 prototype won't make it easy on you, so keep your guard up whenever you're not attacking, and avoid the environmental hazards while you move about the arena.

# Challenge 4

| Requirement | Opponent | Level | Objective |
|---|---|---|---|
| Grand Master Difficulty | EG-4 Prototype | Droid Lab | Defeat the opponent. Use all five combos, Dark Blast, and a Charged Combo. |

"EG" droids are not easy to contend with on Padawan or Jedi Knight difficulty levels. On Grand Master difficulty, they are one of the hardest enemies in the game. This is one of the hardest challenges in the entire game, so prepare for some white-knuckle dueling. At the battle's start, immediately fire a Dark Blast. Unlike other challenges, even the easier combos become difficult against this opponent, so get those out of the way first. If you attempt to execute the harder combos first, you'll fail, since the other droid is much more aggressive.

Because the droid is more aggressive, you can parry more often and fill your Force Gauge more quickly. As soon as its full, execute your Charged Combo. With two tasks and two or three combos complete in the first round, you need only execute the remaining combos in the second round. If you fail to fill your Force Gauge in round one, don't worry. You'll be able to fill it halfway through round two.

# Battle Mode

## Versus General Grievous

**Battle Arena:** Raxus Prime

General Grievous is a tough fighter, but with no Force talents and a far more evasive fighting style, you should be able to quickly overwhelm him with several combos. Bully Grievous around the arena and follow him as he jumps around. Smack him with short combos as he lands, then knock him off the arena to set him up for an ambush assault.

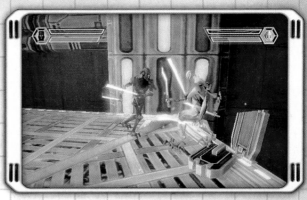

## Versus Plo Koon

**Battle Arena:** Sarlacc Pit

Like Grievous, Plo Koon can be cornered, bullied, and knocked off the bridge. However, Koon is far better than Grievous at counterattacking, so don't give Koon any chances to counter by executing wild combos and rushing past the Jedi. Keep control of your 'sabers and let Koon create openings for you as he tries to chip away at your health.

## Versus Mace Windu

**Battle Arena:** Mustafar

Mace Windu is a smart fighter. Rather than go toe-to-toe with you, he continuously stays on the move and uses the environment to his advantage. In round one, he'll often leap behind the ship at the platform's center or hurl debris to keep you at bay. Keep your guard up as you close in, then strike with lots of quick combos once he's within reach of your sword.

# Versus Kit Fisto

**Battle Arena:** Droid Factory

To defeat Kit Fisto, keep moving constantly and use strong sweeping strikes like Smash attacks and Saber Storm. Fisto will try to stay out of reach like Windu but will attack less often. If he tries to leap away, use Dark Blast attacks to knock him off his feet as he lands, then rush in to deliver the blow! Maintain a safe distance from him, but always keep him within reach of your blades.

# Versus EG-05 Jedi Hunter Droid

**Battle Arena:** Separatist Listening Post

In this battle, the environment can be a great ally. Your doppelganger has the same skills and abilities as you, so don't be surprised if it's very fast and hard to parry. Use your strongest combos and lots of leaping attacks. Don't use Dark Blast too often; your foe will simply sidestep the bolt and counter with great accuracy. Watch the environment to keep from frying your own servos and instead try to maneuver the other droid into harm's way.

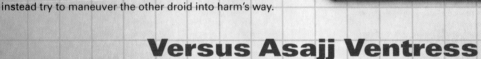

# Versus Asajj Ventress

**Battle Arena:** The Malevolence

Ventress is fast and very similar to you in some ways. She'll often try to stay in constant motion, making it very difficult to string together chains of combos. Knock her down with Smash attacks, Dark Blasts, and leaping slashes, then pounce on her as she gets to her feet. If she tries to attack, block her blows, back away, then reengage her as she approaches you. If you chase her around the arena, she'll slowly chip away at your health until you're a pile of spare parts. Make her fight your fight and you'll win every time.

# General Grievous

## Vitals

**Allegiance:** Separatist

**Rank:** Supreme General

**Class:** Jedi Hunter

**Species:** Kaleesh Cyborg

**Height:** 2.03

**Saber color:** Wields four 'sabers, two blue and two green

**Banter style:** Overconfident, malicious, and crafty

**Special attack:** Saber Onslaught

**Initial Force Energy:** N/A

**Potential Force Energy:** N/A

## Stats

| Force Attacks | Combos | Force Energy | Agility | Special |
|---|---|---|---|---|
| 5 | 3 | 0 | 1 | Saber Onslaught |

## Bio

During the Clone Wars, Grievous emerged as one of Count Dooku's apprentices and right-hand droid. Suffering near-fatal injuries that rendered his body useless, or so he was told, Grievous was disgusted by his new droid body and took Dooku's appointment as Supreme Commander of the droid armies as an insult. Grievous, however, would soon come to highly respect Dooku and Sidious as the Confederacy's only political leadership.

## Alternate Costumes

**Standard**

**Alternate**

**Kaleesh Markings**

**Supreme General Battle Gear**

**Sith Markings**

# Fighting Style

General Grievous is a cagey character. He's surprisingly light on his feet for a large walking pile of bolts and is extremely dangerous with all four 'sabers. He has no Force Energy abilities, so he relies solely on his lightsaber skills and Force attacks. Once he's charged his Force Combo Gauge, he'll quickly unleash his signature attack. His other special attack, Saber Onslaught, is always a threat to knock opponents off the arena.

## Combos

| Signature Move | Difficulty | 1st Hit | 2nd Hit | 3rd Hit | 4th Hit | Shares Combo with... |
|---|---|---|---|---|---|---|
| Saber Storm | Easy | L | R | L | — | Asajj Ventress and EG-05 Jedi Hunter |
| Warrior Slayer | Easy | R | L | R | -- | N/A |
| Great Jedi Purge | Hard | U | L | D | S | N/A |
| War-Cry of the Kaleesh | Hard | U | D | R | U | N/A |
| Jedi Hunter | Hard | L | D | S | U | N/A |

# Challenge Mode

## Challenge 1

| Requirement | Opponent | Level | Objective |
| --- | --- | --- | --- |
| Jedi Knight Difficulty | Ahsoka Tano | Sky Station | Defeat the opponent and knock her off the level at least three times. |

### CHALLENGER'S MOTIVATION

Grievous knows he can outpower the young Jedi Padawan; however, Ahsoka is quick. Her shiftiness, speed, and ability to maneuver around Grievous infuriates the general, as he cannot easily defeat such a tricky target.

Ahsoka is far too fast to pin against the arena's edge. Luckily, your Saber Onslaught has a long range. With it, you can begin your attack from a distance, rush toward Tano, pummel her with your 'sabers, and knock her off the platform with your final blow. Tano is shifty, though, and can often sidestep or leap over your attack, so launch your Saber Onslaught from a moderate distance. If you miss, she'll sidestep and follow up with a combo while you're wheezing to catch your breath.

As you fight, Tano will dart back and forth around the arena, making her extremely hard to hit. However, if you corner her against the arena's edge, use Smash attacks to knock her off the platform. After knocking her off three times, finish her off with quick combos and plenty of counterattacks.

## Challenge 2

| Requirement | Opponent | Level | Objective |
| --- | --- | --- | --- |
| Jedi Knight Difficulty | Kit Fisto | Mustafar | Defeat the opponent, using three combos and three parry attacks. |

### CHALLENGER'S MOTIVATION

Grievous is always looking to add another Jedi lightsaber to his collection by murdering Jedi across the galaxy. Kit Fisto's 'saber would look great in Grievous's collection.

Jedi Master Fisto is an easy duelist to parry. His 'saber strikes are short, controlled, and often easier to anticipate than other more aggressive fighters' attacks. Maintain your guard during the battle and wait for Fisto to attack. Immediately after parrying and knocking the Jedi off balance, follow up with short combos like Saber Storm or Warrior Slayer.

If you are patient and act quickly when the opportunity arises, you should be able to execute each of your three combos after parrying every time. Once you've taken care of the challenge requirements, defeat Fisto with lots of short combos and counters.

STAR WARS
THE
CLONE
WARS

LIGHTSABER DUELS

PRIMA OFFICIAL GAME GUIDE

# Challenge 3

| Requirement | Opponent | Level | Objective |
|---|---|---|---|
| Jedi Knight Difficulty | Obi-Wan Kenobi | The Malevolence | Defeat the opponent and get to the last car before the attack trains pull up with yours. |

### CHALLENGER'S MOTIVATION

Obi-Wan's wartime exploits made him one of the most famous Jedi in the galaxy. This earned the attention of the Separatist general Grievous, who wanted to add both Anakin's and Obi-Wan's lightsabers to his belt as trophies.

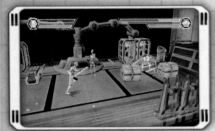

Of all of Grievous's challenges, this may be the easiest. When the first round begins, use Saber Storm to knock Obi-Wan away and rush past him. Jump over the crates and obstacles on the right and continue jumping right until you reach the tram's far end. Don't bother fighting Kenobi as you go. Instead, focus on immediately drawing the fight to the front of the train.

After you reach the front of the train, use a series of Saber Onslaught, Smash attacks, and short combos to strike down the Jedi general. It shouldn't take more than a minute and a half to reach the front, thus meeting your challenge requirement.

# Challenge 4

| Requirement | Opponent | Level | Objective |
|---|---|---|---|
| Jedi Knight Difficulty | Mace Windu | Droid Factory | Defeat the opponent. Use all five combos and at least one Charged Combo. |

### CHALLENGER'S MOTIVATION

Mace Windu Force-crushed the plates covering Grievous's internal organs, severely damaging his lungs. This crippling blow injured Grievous for the rest of his life. The encounter with Windu damaged his body and might have left a scar on his psyche as well. Grievous would happily exact revenge on Windu when given the opportunity.

Mace Windu is a difficult opponent to execute all five combos against, but with a little patience, a healthy dose of parrying and sidestepping, and good combo skills, you can successfully finish this challenge. Of all the other Jedi Masters, Windu is the most aggressive, allowing you more opportunities to parry his attacks. After deflecting his blows with a parry, follow it up with short combos like Warrior Slayer or Saber Storm.

The other three combos, all of which are harder to perform, are best executed after sidestepping the Jedi's blows or leaping over and landing behind him. After executing all five combos and parrying a few blows, your Force Gauge should be full and ready to unleash a Charged Combo. Do so to finish him off and successfully complete your final challenge.

# Battle Mode

## Versus Asajj Ventress

**Battle Arena:** Raxus Prime

The battle against Ventress can be very fun. Her dual lightsaber style matches up very well against your multi-'saber techniques. Rush Ventress with Saber Onslaught and knock her off the platform. As she recovers, hit her with Jedi Hunter and War-Cry of the Kaleesh to sever huge chunks off her Health bar.

## Versus Ahsoka Tano

**Battle Arena:** Sarlacc Pit

In this small arena, Ahsoka doesn't have anywhere to run. The bridge is too small for her to continuously evade your attacks, and the Sarlacc tentacles can potentially knock her off her feet and slow her down. Be extra aggressive during this battle and slash at the pint-sized Padawan with your strongest combos. Pin her against the arena's edge and pummel her.

## Versus Kit Fisto

**Battle Arena:** Mustafar

Master Fisto can be taken quickly with a flurry of strong combos. He's a much more defensive fighter, meaning he'll try to block and parry more often, but that is also his greatest weakness. If you use stab attacks and leaping slashes, you can open him up for stronger, more devastating combos. Apply pressure on the Jedi and don't let up until he's on the ground.

# Versus Anakin Skywalker

**Battle Arena:** Droid Factory

Anakin Skywalker is a tough opponent. He's a great balanced fighter who complements his lightsaber skills with great use of Force powers like Force Blast. Parry his lightsaber blows and counter consistently. To get clean shots on the brooding Jedi, dodge his Force Blasts and strike him from his flank. As he staggers, follow up with Great Jedi Purge and Jedi Hunter.

# Versus General Grievous

**Battle Arena:** Droid Lab

The battle against your other self can be quick and painless. You match up perfectly with your twin, so don't worry about who is faster or more agile. Instead, use your multi-'saber attacks to overwhelm the other Grievous. If he attacks with Saber Onslaught, sidestep his attack, wait until he's wheezing and vulnerable, then attack with War-Cry of the Kaleesh.

# Versus Mace Windu

**Battle Arena:** The Negotiator

Mace Windu is a great test for your skills. He's a strong fighter with great combo skills. Watch out for his Achieved Focus and Vaapad Strike attack, which he'll land with deadly efficiency. Keep him from performing his favorite combos by parrying a lot. If he lands the first blow in his combo, immediately parry the second, or even the third. During the first round, step behind the equipment and other electrical components to create obstacles for the Jedi, then pounce on him as he approaches. In the second round, take the fight to the center walkway to restrict his movement.

# Kit Fisto

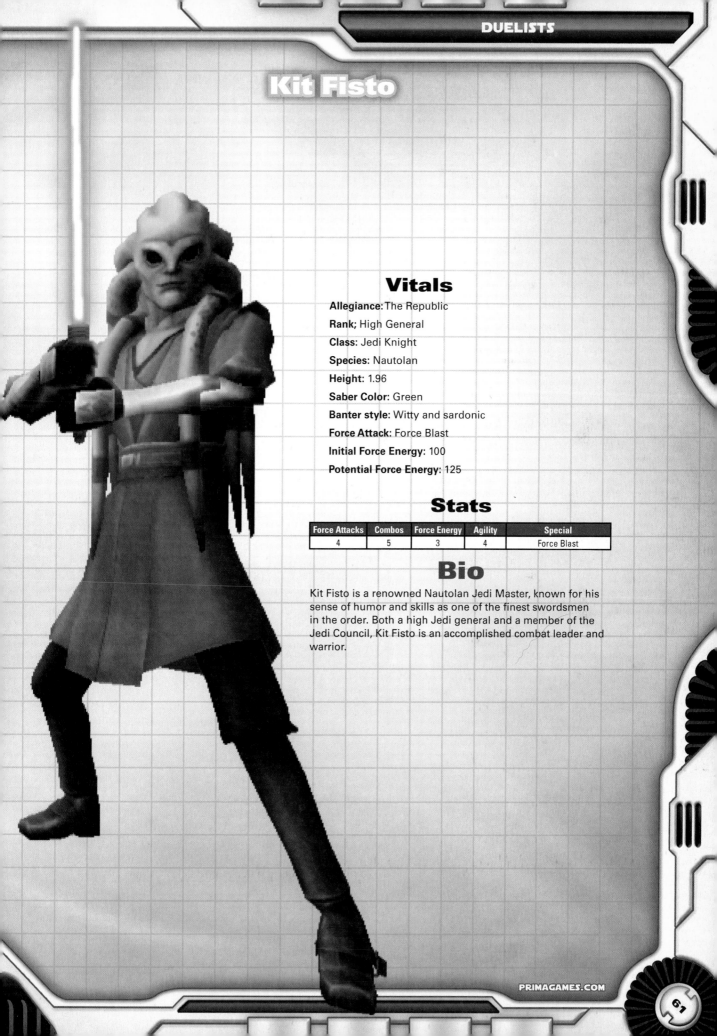

## Vitals

**Allegiance:** The Republic

**Rank;** High General

**Class:** Jedi Knight

**Species:** Nautolan

**Height:** 1.96

**Saber Color:** Green

**Banter style:** Witty and sardonic

**Force Attack:** Force Blast

**Initial Force Energy:** 100

**Potential Force Energy:** 125

## Stats

| Force Attacks | Combos | Force Energy | Agility | Special |
|---|---|---|---|---|
| 4 | 5 | 3 | 4 | Force Blast |

## Bio

Kit Fisto is a renowned Nautolan Jedi Master, known for his sense of humor and skills as one of the finest swordsmen in the order. Both a high Jedi general and a member of the Jedi Council, Kit Fisto is an accomplished combat leader and warrior.

# Fighting Style

## Alternate Costumes

**Standard**

**Alternate**

**Jedi Task Force Robes**

**High General Robe**

**Jedi Council Robe**

Being a master of the same lightsaber form as Ahsoka Tano, Kit Fisto can perform more advanced versions of her attacks. He's agile, has strong combos, and makes frequent use of Force attacks.

## Combos

| Signature Move | Difficulty | 1st Hit | 2nd Hit | 3rd Hit | 4th Hit | Shares Combo with... |
|---|---|---|---|---|---|---|
| Shii-Cho Storm | Easy | L | R | D | — | N/A |
| Insightful Strike | Easy | R | L | U | — | N/A |
| Nautolan's Torrent | Medium | U | L | D | U | N/A |
| Amphibious Assault | Medium | D | U | R | D | N/A |
| Focused Offense | Hard | R | D | L | U | Obi-Wan Kenobi and Anakin Skywalker |

# Challenge Mode

## Challenge 1

| Requirement | Opponent | Level | Objective |
|---|---|---|---|
| Jedi Knight Difficulty | General Grievous | Raxus Prime | Defeat the opponent within three minutes. |

**CHALLENGER'S MOTIVATION**

Kit Fisto and his former Padawan Nahdar Vebb, confronted Grievous at his lair on the Vassek moon. Kit knows that the general is not a force to be taken lightly.

In order to complete this challenge successfully, be very aggressive. Grievous will be evasive and very frenetic throughout the match, so keep up with him and stay constantly on the attack. Dodge his Saber Onslaught by leaping over it and counterattack from behind. As he's down, use an upward Smash attack to deliver even more damage.

If Grievous attempts to evade your attacks by leaping away, use jumping Force attacks to slash the bucket of bolts back down to the ground. As he lands, continue your assault and melt his armor.

## Challenge 2

| Requirement | Opponent | Level | Objective |
|---|---|---|---|
| Jedi Knight Difficulty | EG-3 Prototype | The Malevolence | Defeat the opponent and use at least one Charged Combo. |

**CHALLENGER'S MOTIVATION**

Kit Fisto needs no motivation to destroy the EG-3 Prototype. Because the droid is programmed to hunt down all Jedi Knights, destroying it is a matter of survival.

The most difficult thing about this challenge is filling your Force Gauge to unleash the Charged Combo. There are crates between you and the droid; as soon as the battle begins, Force Throw these crates at it. If you're fast enough, you may be able to throw two crates and begin filling your Force Gauge immediately. Continue building your charge by spinning the droid around and landing quick combos like Shii-Cho Storm.

Once your gauge is full, hit the Sith puppet with your Charged Combo. After fulfilling the challenge requirement, you can safely finish the droid off with strong combos and leaping slashes.

# Challenge 3

| Requirement | Opponent | Level | Objective |
|---|---|---|---|
| Jedi Knight Difficulty | Asajj Ventress | Droid Factory | Defeat the opponent and use all five combos. |

### CHALLENGER'S MOTIVATION

Kit Fisto and Ventress once battled to the brink of death. Ventress hates Jedi and has made it her duty to rid the galaxy of them in order to gain Count Dooku's praises. Kit Fisto cannot let Ventress continue hunting Jedi for the Separatists.

Ventress is extremely fast, making it difficult to connect with all five of your combos. Luckily, all you have to do is connect with each combo once. Begin by rushing toward Dooku's lackey and breaking her defense with a stab attack. As soon as she's off balance, follow up with Focused Offense. With the toughest combo to execute out of the way, whittle away at the bald baddy with Nautolan's Torrent and Amphibious Assault.

Leave Shii-Cho Storm and Insightful Strike for the second (and possibly third) round. If you manage to land one but not the other, feel free to throw the second round and execute the final combo during the third and final round. There are no time limits, so your main concern is connecting with the final blow, at the very least, of all five combos.

# Challenge 4

| Requirement | Opponent | Level | Objective |
|---|---|---|---|
| Grand Master Difficulty | Count Dooku | Droid Lab | Defeat the opponent and destroy the two astromech droids. |

### CHALLENGER'S MOTIVATION

Kit knows the danger represented by Count Dooku and is another Jedi who wants to bring the dark side of the Force to justice.

The trickiest part of this challenge is destroying both astromech droids. You must destroy one droid per round, as there is only one droid available at a time. As you fight Dooku, run around the entire arena to locate the droid. When you do, duck behind the droid so it is between you and Dooku. Slash the astromech a few times until it blows up, then focus your efforts on Dooku.

In the second round, do the same thing. Locate the droid and slash it before you finish off Dooku. If you finish the fight with the count before destroying the second droid, you'll fail the challenge.

# Battle Mode

## Versus Mace Windu

**Battle Arena:** Raxus Prime

Windu is a great combo specialist and is very strong. Parry his attacks to build your Force charge, then assail him with Charged Combos. Stay light on your feet and constantly on the move to throw off Windu's combos. Spring on the Jedi Master from the sides and behind to open up with combo chains.

## Versus Count Dooku

**Battle Arena:** Sarlacc Pit

Dooku is the perfect opponent for you. His propensity to block and parry make your great combos difficult to execute, but his slow pace makes your speed a great advantage. Dash around the count's defense and attack him from behind and the sides. If you come at him head-on, he'll parry your blows and counter. Circumvent his defense with your speed!

## Versus Obi-Wan Kenobi

**Battle Arena:** Mustafar

Fighting against Obi-Wan is a test of technical lightsaber skill. He's a super balanced fighter who slightly favors Force powers, making this a great test of your Jedi skills. Approach this battle with a balance between 'saber skills, Force attacks, and defense. Don't be too aggressive or Kenobi will quickly make you pay with his strong combo skills. Instead, pick your slashes carefully and parry as much as possible.

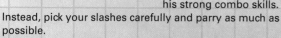

## Versus Asajj Ventress

**Battle Arena:** Droid Factory

Speed is the name of the game against Asajj Ventress. Overwhelm her with speed and a flurry of short two- and three-hit combos to whittle her down. Once she's down to less than 50 percent health, use Charged Combos, Shii-Cho Storm, and Insightful Strikes to finish her off.

## Versus Kit Fisto

**Battle Arena:** Tatooine

Facing Kit Fisto is a lot like facing Obi-Wan Kenobi. Fight a balanced fight, but favor your lightsaber skills a bit more. Execute combos regularly, but defend against your clone's attacks. Remember, you're fighting your twin, so your strengths are his strengths. Take away his ability to execute combos by blocking and parrying his attacks, and rob him of his speed by keeping him on his back. Strong combos and a fair amount of defense spell out a surefire win.

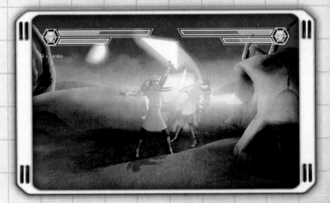

## Versus EG-05 Jedi Hunter Droid

**Battle Arena:** The Malevolence

The Jedi hunter droid is dangerous. It's got raw power, great 'saber skills, and enough speed to make you dizzy. When facing it, increase your attack rate. Don't go for lots of big combos; instead, whittle away at it with short, quick 'saber strikes. Use your big combos as supplements to a faster fighting style built on short combos. Follow the droid around the arena and chip away at it as you build your Force Gauge. Once the gauge is full, finish off Dooku's droid with a Charged Combo.

# Mace Windu

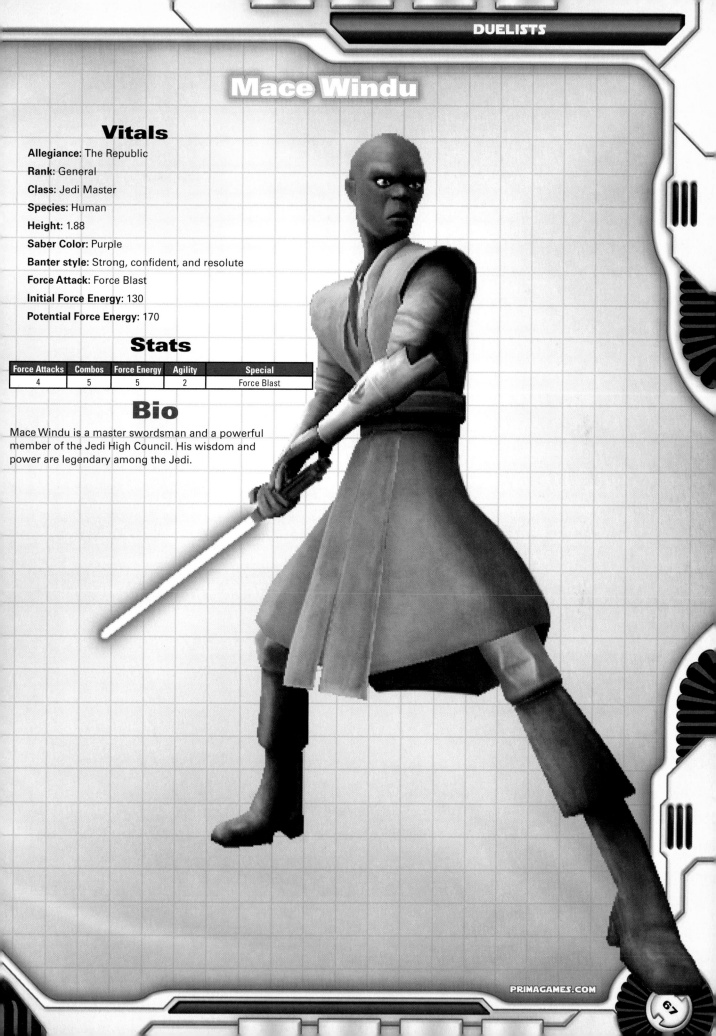

## Vitals

**Allegiance:** The Republic

**Rank:** General

**Class:** Jedi Master

**Species:** Human

**Height:** 1.88

**Saber Color:** Purple

**Banter style:** Strong, confident, and resolute

**Force Attack:** Force Blast

**Initial Force Energy:** 130

**Potential Force Energy:** 170

## Stats

| Force Attacks | Combos | Force Energy | Agility | Special |
|:---:|:---:|:---:|:---:|:---:|
| 4 | 5 | 5 | 2 | Force Blast |

## Bio

Mace Windu is a master swordsman and a powerful member of the Jedi High Council. His wisdom and power are legendary among the Jedi.

# Fighting Style

## Alternate Costumes

**Standard**

**Alternate**

**Jedi Task Force Robes**

**Jedi Master Robe**

**Jedi Council Robe**

Mace Windu uses a devastating lightsaber form that borders on the edge of falling to the dark side. Only his mastery and concentration on the light side prevented him from succumbing to his own anger.

## Combos

| Signature Move | Difficulty | 1st Hit | 2nd Hit | 3rd Hit | 4th Hit | Shares Combo with... |
|---|---|---|---|---|---|---|
| Vaapad Strike | Medium | R | L | D | U | N/A |
| Achieved Focus | Medium | D | R | U | D | N/A |
| Judgment Strike | Hard | L | U | R | D | N/A |
| Path of the Righteous | Hard | U | R | D | L | Plo Koon |
| Hurikane Onslaught | Hard | R | U | L | U | N/A |

# Challenge Mode

## Challenge 1

| Requirement | Opponent | Level | Objective |
| --- | --- | --- | --- |
| Jedi Knight Difficulty | Ahsoka Tano | The Resolute | Defeat the opponent within three minutes. |

### CHALLENGER'S MOTIVATION

Mace sees in Ahsoka the same sense of defiance he sees in her teacher. Through no fault of her own, Mace has the same distrust of Anakin's Padawan as he does for Anakin.

The battle against Ahsoka Tano can be tough. Her speed and shiftiness make her a very difficult opponent to pin down. She'll often leap over you, sidestep, and roll away from attacks, and even launch quick combos as she speeds around the arena and makes herself a difficult target. As she evades your close-quarter attacks, don't let up. Begin your attacks from afar as she moves toward you so that the final blow in your combos connects.

Use Charged Combos to take big chunks off her Health bar. She'll frequently try to flank you, so intercept her attacks, parry, and counter. As long as you're also constantly on the offensive, you can dispatch her in less than three minutes.

## Challenge 2

| Requirement | Opponent | Level | Objective |
| --- | --- | --- | --- |
| Jedi Knight Difficulty | Count Dooku | The Tranquility | Defeat the opponent and avoid the Tabana Gas blasts. |

### CHALLENGER'S MOTIVATION

It is said that only his one-time friend Dooku and the venerable Grand Master Yoda could outspar Mace Windu.

The battle against Count Dooku isn't very hard, actually. You can take him out handily with lots of Judgment Strikes, Serenity of Light, and Whirlwind of Justice attacks. During the first round, defeat Dooku as you would in any other fight. Break through his defense by leaping above and slashing from behind or stabbing through it, then following with any of the above combos.

During the second round, keep the fight on the ship's far left side. Do not move toward the center or you'll risk destroying the console near the arena's middle. However, once the console is destroyed, the ship begins to unleash several gas blasts that make it difficult to complete the challenge. Keep Dooku near the far left and assault him with plenty of Smash attacks to keep him on his back.

# Challenge 3

| Requirement | Opponent | Level | Objective |
|---|---|---|---|
| Jedi Knight Difficulty | General Grievous | The Negotiator | Defeat the opponent and do not lose more than 25 percent health. |

### CHALLENGER'S MOTIVATION

Mace Windu Force-crushed the plates covering Grievous's internal organs, severely damaging his lungs. This crippling blow injured Grievous for life and caused his severe coughing and wheezing fits. Mace is always willing to finish the job he started.

This challenge is very similar to the Dooku challenge. Instead of avoiding an obstacle during the second round, however, you must keep from losing more than 25 percent health (one-fourth of your Health bar). During the first round, defeat Grievous as you would during any other fight. Pummel him with combos as he tries to leap away and corner him against the arena's edge to keep him from escaping.

During the second round, you must become very evasive and keep up your guard consistently. Parry as much as possible to keep from taking damage, and build up your Force Gague. Stay on the move and only use your Charged Combos when you're sure you'll get clean hits. If your Charged Combo misses, Grievous can easily follow up with Saber Onslaught, ruining your challenge.

### NOTE

Because the Health bar is not measured in percentages, visualize the bar split into four pieces.

# Challenge 4

| Requirement | Opponent | Level | Objective |
|---|---|---|---|
| Grand Master Difficulty | Anakin Skywalker | Separatist Listening Post | Defeat the opponent within three minutes and use all five combos. |

### CHALLENGER'S MOTIVATION

Despite Anakin's bravery, Mace Windu was reluctant to allow him into the Jedi High Council. Mace was careful about who his friends were and who he trusted. Despite the fact that Anakin Skywalker was one of the most talented Jedi in the order, Windu stated that he did not fully trust him and wasn't convinced that Anakin was the Chosen One.

By far Windu's most difficult challenge, he must defeat Anakin in three minutes with all five combos. Anakin is a smart fighter, and his ability to counter nearly every attack makes it difficult for your combos to connect. In fact, Anakin can nearly always parry the second blow of any of your combos. If you don't execute the combos correctly and quickly, he'll parry and counter until he defeats you.

The key to winning this challenge is keeping your combo motions fluid and quick! Don't pause between combo strokes or you'll give Skywalker the perfect chance to turn the tables. If you still struggle to connect with your combos consistently, begin them a few steps away from Anakin and connect with the third or fourth hits. Don't bother with smaller two- or three-hit combos during this battle. After you land all five combos, execute Charged Combos to take off huge chunks of his health. Stick to your most powerful combos (any of your signature five and Charged Combos) and you'll fell the cocky Jedi within three minutes.

# Battle Mode

## Versus Kit Fisto

**Battle Arena:** Raxus Prime

Kit Fisto is a fun opponent. His speed and combo skills make him a great test of your combo abilities. Use the arena's wide-open space to formulate long combo chains, and use the debris scattered about to hit Fisto from afar. Once your Charged Combo is ready, let it loose and take down the big green Jedi.

## Versus Asajj Ventress

**Battle Arena:** Sarlacc Pit

Ventress is a fast fighter. She uses her speed and dual 'sabers to overwhelm her enemies and slice them up with short combo flurries. Take away her ability to string together combos by pinning her against the edge of the bridge. If she tries to evade, use Smash attacks to knock her off the bridge and immediately slash her as she returns to the battle.

## Versus Plo Koon

**Battle Arena:** Mustafar

The battle against Plo Koon can often play out like a game of cat and mouse. Koon, like Tano, is light on his feet and will often dart around the arena evasively. Chase the dodgy Jedi around the arena and knock him off his feet with Smash attacks. Once he's back up, immediately follow up with strong combos to take him out. During the first round, use the electrical generators around the arena to inflict more damage on Koon. In the second round, the uneven terrain make it a great place to set up ambush attacks and Smash attacks.

# Versus Count Dooku

**Battle Arena:** Droid Factory

Because Dooku is a master blocker and a great defensive swordsman, you must first break through his defense to connect with follow-up blows. The odd, T-shaped arena makes it a great place to corner Dooku and keep him from defending against your attacks. Follow the count around, break through his defense with stab attacks, and force him into a niche. Once he's cornered, hit him with your strongest combos.

Vaapad Strike

# Versus Mace Windu

**Battle Arena:** The Negotiator

The fight against your doppelganger boils down to who is more skilled with the lightsaber. During the first round, there are many pieces of equipment to use as projectiles, so the occasional Force Throw might come into play. But without proper combos and 'saber skills, thrown objects don't do much. Overpower your other self by stringing together signature attacks like Whirlwind of Justice and Judgment Strike with short two- and three-hit combos. In the second round, forget about using the Force and instead use more Charged Combos.

Smash Attack          Force Blast

# Versus General Grievous

**Battle Arena:** Droid Lab

The Droid Lab is a great arena in which to face General Grievous. The crates scattered about make perfect weapons to hit him from afar as he leaps around and simultaneously fill your Force Gauge. Once the reactor begins to go haywire, you can use the electrical currents to zap Grievous and hold him in place while you formulate your next attack. Use a heavy dose of projectiles, Charged Combos, and Smash attacks to destroy Dooku's demented drone.

# Obi-Wan Kenobi

## Vitals

**Allegiance:** The Republic

**Rank:** General

**Class:** Jedi Master

**Species:** Human

**Height:** 1.8

**Saber Color:** Blue

**Banter style:** Dry, witty, and debonair

**Force Attack:** Force Blast

**Initial Force Energy:** 130

**Potential Force Energy:** 170

## Stats

| Force Attacks | Combos | Force Energy | Agility | Special |
|:---:|:---:|:---:|:---:|:---:|
| 2 | 5 | 4 | 3 | Force Blast |

## Bio

A dedicated and decorated Jedi Master, Obi-Wan is determined to see the Jedi Council effectively deal with the Separatist threat and uphold the unity of the Republic.

## Alternate Costumes

**Standard**

**Alternate**

**ARC Battle Gear**

**Tatooine Battle Gear**

**Kashyyyk Battle Gear**

## Fighting Style

Using honored Jedi Knight lightsaber styles, Obi-Wan themes his attacks with flourish and counter strikes.

## Combos

| Signature Move | Difficulty | 1st Hit | 2nd Hit | 3rd Hit | 4th Hit | Shares Combo with... |
|---|---|---|---|---|---|---|
| Strength of Soresu | Easy | L | R | L | R | N/A |
| Rise of Virtue | Easy | R | L | R | D | Ahsoka Tano |
| Ataru Surge | Medium | R | U | U | — | N/A |
| Eye of the Storm | Medium | U | D | L | — | N/A |
| Focused Offense | Hard | R | D | L | U | Anakin Skywalker and Kit Fisto |

# Challenge Mode

## Challenge 1

| Requirement | Opponent | Level | Objective |
|---|---|---|---|
| Jedi Knight Difficulty | Asajj Ventress | Teth Castle Dungeon | Defeat the opponent within three minutes. |

### CHALLENGER'S MOTIVATION

Obi-Wan has a conflicted relationship with Ventress; he knows she's the enemy, but he also feels that she's been led astray and can be turned. He needles her with flirtatious comments, meant to prod her into acting rashly. Through numerous battles with Ventress, Obi-Wan has found out much about her past and believes that there is still some good in her.

When the fight begins, immediately leap to action. Ventress is a dodgy fighter and can stay on the move throughout the entire battle, making your time limit hard to hit. Keep her within your reach by using long-distance assaults like stab attacks and by Force Throwing objects at her. Once you reach the bald assassin, rush her with short combos to chip away at her health.

If she tries launching an attack, sidestep or parry, then counter with two- and three-hit combos. Your more powerful signature attacks are useful, but if you miss the jittering Jedi wannabe, then you'll waste precious time and leave yourself open to counterattack. On the other hand, if you can land signature attacks consistently, the match will be over considerably faster. During this three-minute time limit, consider signature attacks a risk-versus-reward option.

## Challenge 2

| Requirement | Opponent | Level | Objective |
|---|---|---|---|
| Jedi Knight Difficulty | Asajj Ventress | The Resolute | Defeat the opponent and use at least one combo and one Charged Combo. |

### NOTE

Obi-Wan's motivation for defeating Ventress does not change from battle to battle.

With no time limit to worry about, you can take your time setting up your attacks during this challenge. Begin by fulfilling the "one combo" requirement and hit Ventress with Strength of the Soresu. It's the easiest and quickest combo to execute, and it will frequently spin your enemy around. After you execute your one combo, begin to parry Ventress's attacks and hit her with boxes and other junk lying around the arena.

As soon as your Force Gauge is full, unleash your Charged Combo. If it connects, then finish off Dooku's domed drone any way you see fit. If you miss, begin to parry her attacks again and refill your Force Gauge. Remember, you don't have a time limit on this challenge, so if you need a third round to complete the challenge requirements, you can always throw the second round.

**LIGHTSABER DUELS**

PRIMA OFFICIAL GAME GUIDE

# Challenge 3

| Requirement | Opponent | Level | Objective |
| --- | --- | --- | --- |
| Jedi Knight Difficulty | Asajj Ventress | Tatooine | Defeat the opponent, and destroy the teeth and the droids in the battle arena. |

By now, defeating Ventress should be old hat. As soon as the fight begins, move toward the arena's far left side and position yourself behind the four large teeth sprouting from the ground. Wait for Ventress to approach, then execute a sideways slash to cut through one of the teeth and send it flying at your opponent. Carefully edge to the other teeth and do the same until you destroy all four teeth.

After you destroy all four teeth in the first round, dispatch Ventress as you would in any other fight. Since there are no teeth in the secondary arena, you can finish the fight however you want. We suggest you put an end to Ventress with lots of Smash attacks and short combos.

# Challenge 4

| Requirement | Opponent | Level | Objective |
| --- | --- | --- | --- |
| Jedi Knight Difficulty | Asajj Ventress | Sarlacc Pit | Defeat the opponent and knock her off the bridge. |

Since both rounds take place on the bridge, you'll have plenty of opportunities to knock Ventress off. Although she is very quick and evasive, Ventress will often give you plenty of chances to slash her off the bridge after a failed attack. Engage her in battle and wait for her to begin Exar Kun's Assault. When she does, either leap over her or sidestep her approach. When she's done, she'll pause momentarily to catch her breath.

As soon as she does, use a Smash attack to knock her off the bridge. After you meet the challenge requirement, finish the fight by pinning Ventress near the bridge's edge and pummel her with Eye of the Storm, Focused Offense, and a Charged Combo.

# Battle Mode

## Versus Anakin Skywalker

**Battle Arena:** Raxus Prime

Anakin may be a Jedi Knight now, but that doesn't mean you can't still teach your old Padawan a few lessons in lightsaber combat. Use short, controlled lightsaber slashes to slowly chop down Anakin's Health bar and parry to build your Force charge. Use the wide-open arena to evade his attacks, and counter whenever he passes you in a missed slash. Once he's below 50 percent health, bully him off the arena and pounce on him as he rejoins the fight.

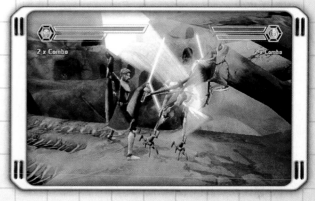

## Versus General Grievous

**Battle Arena:** Sarlacc Pit

Generally Grievous can be a difficult opponent to face in combat. In this arena, however, the advantage is all yours. Your strong combo skills and stout Force Energy abilities make the long, thin bridge a perfect place to keep the cagey general in check. Pin him against the side of the bridge and pummel him with your superior combo skills. When he leaps over you to get out of the corner, turn around and hit him with Force Blast or a stabbing attack to get back within range.

## Versus Plo Koon

**Battle Arena:** Mustafar

Plo Koon is surprisingly effective with Force abilities such as Force Blast and Force Throw. Attack your Jedi colleague with a chain of signature attacks. If he moves out of your range, beat him to the punch and Force Throw objects at him to knock him off balance and rob him of a potential weapon. If you miss with a combo, move out of his range to avoid taking damage from his Force Blast.

# Versus Asajj Ventress

**Battle Arena:** Droid Factory

The fight against Ventress in the Droid Factory can be very difficult. Because Ventress is fast and evasive, the awkwardly shaped arena will often make reaching her difficult. Instead of chasing her around the arena, let her come to you. Stay near the center of the middle walkway or near one of the battleground's edges to take advantage of the wide-open areas. If you are constantly chasing her, she'll slash you to bits as you approach.

# Versus Obi-Wan Kenobi

**Battle Arena:** Teth Castle Ramparts

When facing Obi-Wan Kenobi, balance your lightsaber, Force attacks, and defensive skills evenly as you block, parry, and attack your other self. The Teth Castle Ramparts are riddled with rocks and other debris that you can use to throw at your opponent and set up your combos. However, if you get carried away trying to execute every combo in your repertoire, Obi-Two will simply parry and counter. Remember to keep your guard up when you're a fair distance from your enemy—he can Force Throw rocks too!

# Versus Count Dooku

**Battle Arena:** Separatist Listening Post

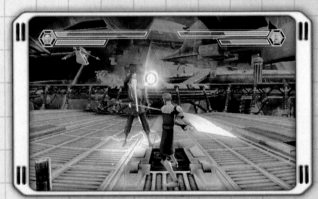

Your final battle is against Dooku. This, much like the previous battle, requires a fair amount of balance. Unlike the battle against the other Obi-Wan, however, Dooku will often remain a bit more defensive. When he does, sidestep, leap, and stab through his 'saber blocks, then unleash quick combos to deal some damage. When he attacks, he'll often try to go for big signature combos. If he connects with the first blow, block the second, then get away from him to keep from taking more damage. Once you're safe, rush in and slash through the gray-bearded baddy.

# Plo Koon

## Vitals

**Allegiance:** The Republic

**Rank:** General

**Class:** Lifetime member of the Jedi Council

**Species:** Kel Dor

**Height:** 1.88

**Saber color:** Blue

**Banter style:** Calm, serious at times

**Force Attack:** Force Blast

**Initial Force Energy:** 130

**Potential Force Energy:** 170

## Stats

| Force Attacks | Combos | Force Energy | Agility | Special |
|:---:|:---:|:---:|:---:|:---:|
| 2 | 3 | 5 | 2 | Force Blast |

## Bio

A wise member of the Jedi Council and general in the Grand Army of the Republic, Plo Koon is also a highly skilled combatant. Having rescued the young Togruta at an early age, Plo Koon shares a special bond with Ahsoka Tano.

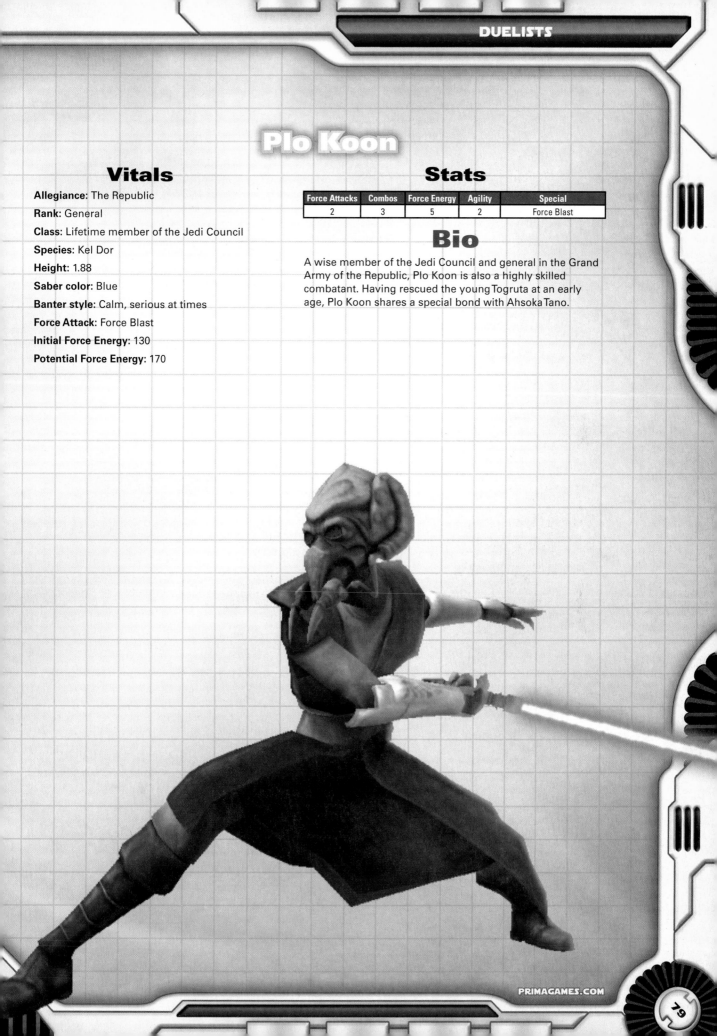

## Alternate Costumes

**Standard**

**Alternate**

**Kel Dorian Robes**

**Jedi Master Robe**

**Jedi Council Robe**

## Fighting Style

Plo Koon is a skilled lightsaber duelist but relies more heavily on his developed Force abilities. With a highly evolved capacity for Force Energy, Koon can augment his lightsaber techniques with Force Blasts and Force-imbued strikes.

## Combos

| Signature Move | Difficulty | 1st Hit | 2nd Hit | 3rd Hit | 4th Hit | Shares Combo with... |
|---|---|---|---|---|---|---|
| Whirlwind of Justice | Medium | R | L | U | R | N/A |
| Tyvokka's Patience | Medium | D | R | L | U | N/A |
| Claw of the Krayt Dragon | Medium | U | D | R | U | N/A |
| Judgment Strike | Hard | L | U | R | D | Mace Windu |
| Serenity of Light | Hard | R | U | L | D | N/A |

# Challenge Mode

## Challenge 1

| Requirement | Opponent | Level | Objective |
|---|---|---|---|
| Padawan Difficulty | General Grievous | Sarlacc Pit | Defeat the opponent and knock him off the bridge. |

### CHALLENGER'S MOTIVATION

Plo Koon knows the dangers General Grievous represents. With Grievous in command of the Separatist droid armies, Koon feels it is his duty as a Jedi for the Republic to stop him.

Plo Koon doesn't have much of an Agility rating, but it is still better than Grievous's Agility rating. And on this small arena, even a one point difference in rating can make a big difference. Grievous will try to outrun you until he can counterattack, but with the bridge being thinner than most fighting areas, you can quickly catch him and run your saber through his servos.

After you catch the cagey creep, throw him off balance with a few combos and finish with a Smash attack. Usually your signature attacks are powerful enough to knock him off the bridge, but with Smash attacks you can increase the chances of sending the Sith wannabe soaring off the bridge.

## Challenge 2

| Requirement | Opponent | Level | Objective |
|---|---|---|---|
| Padawan Difficulty | Count Dooku | The Negotiator | Defeat the opponent and use at least one Charged Combo. |

### CHALLENGER'S MOTIVATION

Plo believes Count Dooku to be nothing more than a traitor to the Jedi, who needs to be brought to justice for his crimes against the Jedi order.

Of your many talents, your exceptionally high Force Energy rating will be your most useful during this challenge. During battle in the first round, use your high Force capacity to Force Throw computer pieces at your enemy. This knocks him off balance and helps charge your Force Gauge quickly. Dooku's attacks are more easily parried than other combatants', also filling your Force Gauge quickly.

Once your Charged Combo is ready, let it loose to fulfill your challenge requirement. When it connects, resume your assault on the traitorous Sith Lord with short combos and Force Energy attacks like Force Thrown objects and Force Blast.

# Challenge 3

| Requirement | Opponent | Level | Objective |
|---|---|---|---|
| Padawan Difficulty | EG-4 Prototype | Droid Lab | Defeat the opponent and avoid the electrical blasts. |

## CHALLENGER'S MOTIVATION

Plo Koon needs no motivation to destroy the EG-4 prototype. Because the droid is programmed to hunt down all Jedi Knights, destroying it is a matter of survival.

This may be Koon's most difficult challenge. Not only must you contend with the speedy EG-4 prototype droid, but you must also do it while avoiding an environmental hazard! The best approach for this fight is to use all five combos during the first round. By doing so, you finish off the droid more quickly, and you save time before the reactor begins to go haywire in the second round.

The more time you have during the second before the reactors begin to malfunction, the less you'll have to worry about getting caught in the electrical current. During the second round, keep a close eye on the conductors in the background. If they begin to draw a charge, immediately lure the droid to the arena's opposite side. Keep the fight in the foreground, as far as possible from the large conductors. Use Charged Combos and signature attacks to defeat the droid, and stay on the move to keep from wandering into the electrical currents!

# Challenge 4

| Requirement | Opponent | Level | Objective |
|---|---|---|---|
| Jedi Knight Difficulty | Asajj Ventress | Raxus Prime | Defeat the opponent within three minutes and use all five combos. |

## CHALLENGER'S MOTIVATION

Even though he knows that Ventress is nothing more than Count Dooku's assassin, he also knows not to underestimate her desire to be one with the dark side. Koon doesn't take Ventress lightly.

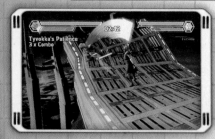
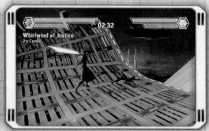

As always, the wide-open arena of Raxus Prime is a great place to execute your signature attacks. Ventress will probably stay at a distance before she attacks, granting you a perfect opportunity to begin your signature combos from afar. As long as the final hit of your combo connects, it counts, so don't stay too close to the shifty Sith puppet or she'll slice you up.

Deliver all five combos quickly! You have only three minutes to defeat her, and if you take too long in fulfilling the challenge requirement, you'll run short on time at the end. Also, refrain from using Smash attacks during this battle, as it will knock her off the arena and waste precious time you need to execute all five combos in three minutes.

# Battle Mode

## Versus Ahsoka Tano

**Battle Arena:** Raxus Prime

Fighting Ahsoka Tano in such a wide-open area can be like trying to snatch a Felucian fruit fly out of the air. She's fast and constantly on the move. Use long-distance attacks like Force Throw and upward Smash attacks to reach the bouncy Padawan, then rush at her with stronger attacks. If she tries to circle around you, turn around, use sideways slash attacks, and follow with signature strikes.

## Versus General Grievous

**Battle Arena:** Sarlacc Pit

Unfortunately for General Grievous, the battle atop the Sarlacc Pit bridge is in your favor. His evasive fighting style is hindered by the bridge's short and thin design. Gash Grievous with strong signature blows, then pin him near the edge of the bridge. As always, knocking him off the bridge with Smash attacks also helps set up stronger combos. Don't let up on the general—overwhelm him with your 'saber and he'll go down like an X-wing with no pilot.

## Versus Asajj Ventress

**Battle Arena:** Mustafar

Ventress will try to use the moderately sized arena to her advantage by utilizing leaping slashes, rolling away, and often leaping back and away from your attacks. Use a similar approach to this fight, just as you did against Tano in the first battle challenge. Attack from a distance with Force Thrown objects and upward Smash attacks. In the second round, you can use the terrain to set up short combos by luring her up stepped areas and around small obstacles.

# Versus EG-05 Jedi Hunter Droid

**Battle Arena:** Droid Factory

Keep the fight near the center walkway of the Droid Factory arena, and use your combos to slice off huge chunks of health from the EG-05 Jedi hunter. If it tries to overpower you with lots of combos and a flurry of 'saber strikes, sidestep, leap, or simply run out of its range, then return with a vengeance. Use Smash attacks to knock the droid off the walkway, and create some breathing room while you formulate your next attack.

# Versus Plo Koon

**Battle Arena:** The Tranquility

During the first round of your mirror battle, use your Force powers to throw anything and everything at your opponent. Slowly build up your Force Gauge so that you can start the second round with a Charged Combo. Start the second round by unleashing your Charged Combo, then destroy the arena's center console to fire up the gas blasts. Pin your enemy against the booster wall, and retreat just as it is about to fire. The blast deals major damage, allowing you to finish off your clone with a few quick combos.

# Versus Count Dooku

**Battle Arena:** Separatist Listening Post

Dooku's greatest strength is his ability to patiently wait for an opening and counter-attack. Use your greatest strength, Force Energy, to break through his defense with thrown objects, then follow it up with quick 'saber strikes. Use short attacks, then back away. If you attempt too many combos, Dooku will parry your blows and counter with deadly accuracy. Instead, slowly chip away at his health with short attacks, then retreat and return a few seconds later with another assault.

A LONG TIME AGO....

In Campaign mode you guide Ahsoka Tano, Anakin Skywalker, and Obi-Wan Kenobi. The following pages detail strategy on how to maximize the Force, sharpen your lightsaber skills, and emerge from the Campaign mode victoriously.

**NOTE**

The following strategy is based on the Padawan difficulty setting.

## The Resolute (Tutorial)

A galaxy at war! Before the Republic can fully mobilize its new clone army, the evil Count Dooku strikes a crippling blow, capturing key hyperspace lanes and isolating the Galactic Senate on Coruscant. On the front lines, Jedi generals Anakin Skywalker and Obi-Wan Kenobi lead their clone troops in a desperate battle against the droid army on Christophsis, aided by Anakin's newly assigned Padawan, Ahsoka Tano.

With the Republic forces victorious, Anakin's flagship, the Resolute, speeds toward its next mission in Hutt space. During the journey, Anakin begins training his young Padawan, uncertain if he is ready for the responsibility....

**NOTE**

Before engaging in Campaign mode, you must complete Beginner Training.

## Beginner Training

### Basic Movement

Great lightsaber duelists understand that proper footwork lays the groundwork for successful battle, so that is where Anakin Skywalker begins his training. As Ahsoka Tano, follow Anakin's instructions and use the control stick on the Wii Nunchuck to move around the Resolute cargo bay.

Move left and right, then back and forth. Acquaint yourself with three-dimensional movement while locked on to your opponent. Accustom yourself to moving while locked on to a target, moving in and out of your opponent's range, and sidestepping. All of these skills will mean the difference between utilizing the Force and becoming one with the Force—permanently.

### Basic Lightsaber Attacks

Any youngling can pick up a lightsaber, often with disastrous results, but it takes a trained hand to properly wield one. Follow Anakin's lead and make short, yet precise, slashing motions with the Wii Remote. First swing the remote from left to right, then right to left. Don't proceed until you make both sideways slashing attacks successfully. When practicing these most basic attacks, don't allow your hand to wander farther than needed to execute the attack. Make the slashes short, swift, and assertive.

Once you've mastered the sideways slash attacks, apply the same short, swift movements to upward and downward slash attacks. Finally, perform a short, forward stabbing motion with the Wii Remote, poking the air in front of you. This performs a lightsaber stab that quickly runs your glowing blade at the opponent's torso and breaks their defenses.

**TIP**

While slashing attacks are the building blocks of your basic fighting style, stabbing attacks are the building blocks of a slightly more advanced fighting technique. For more advanced combat tactics, including how to properly incorporate stabbing attacks and how to create combos, see the "Advanced Combat Techniques" section of the Controls chapter.

## Dodging and Evasive Maneuvers

You can stand against an opponent. You can even take a blow or two. But only a fool would face an enemy and take the brunt of every attack without trying to evade their advances. Anakin knows that even as strong and gifted as he is, he cannot bully through a battle. Listen to his instructions and familiarize yourself with evasive rolls and leaping dodge attempts.

Just as with the basic lightsaber attacks training, execute several evasive maneuvers to get yourself accustomed to moving in real space. Roll forward, leap backward, and execute evasive sideways rolls until you're comfortable that you can escape the enemy's attacks.

## Blocking

Like evasive maneuvers, blocking is just as important as attacking. Raise your 'saber and wait for Anakin to attack. Hold your position and wait for his attack to harmlessly deflect away. When it does, the lesson is over.

Though this may be one of the easiest lessons to learn in Beginner Training, it may be one of the most important. It is extremely easy to get caught up in your offensive assault. After all, great duelists use the Force intuitively and plan ahead, formulating their attacks before they execute. In doing so, you can often get carried away while attacking and forget to block.

# Intermediate Training
## Utilizing the Force

Force-imbued lightsaber attacks are a secondary type of attack. While you can win a duel by using only basic lightsaber attacks, you greatly expand your fighting repertoire by using Force-imbued lightsaber attacks. As Anakin explains, the Force augments your abilities. When harnessed, the Force can make a weak person powerful, a slow person faster, and a mediocre lightsaber duelist a fearsome warrior.

Practice your Force 'saber attacks, and note the distance from which you can lunge toward your opponent and strike. When executed, the Force 'saber strikes allow you to bravely lunge toward your enemy and spin him or her completely around. Of course, you won't always reach your target with your first attack. So take this opportunity to see from just how far you can strike with a Force 'saber strike.

**NOTE**

Each combatant is unique. So while you can only really learn Ahsoka's striking distance, you can still get a very good idea of what other combatants will be capable of.

## Utilizing the Force

Scattered amidst nearly every battle arena are debris, cargo crates, and other movable objects. Like your lightsaber, all of these objects can be used as weapons! The Jedi are always mindful of their surroundings and frequently utilize everything at their disposal to win a battle, and so should you. Follow Anakin's instructions and use the Force to hurl the two crates in the cargo bay at your master.

## Composed Attack and Signature Attacks

With the basics down and a firm grasp of slightly more advanced techniques, you're ready to try your hand at Composed attacks. Composed attacks are 'saber strikes linked together to compose short combos. Though there

are several signature attack combos like Ahsoka's Shii-Cho Slash attack, your fighting style should heavily incorporate basic Composed attacks. Follow Anakin's instructions to learn the basic two-hit combo.

After mastering the two-hit combo, expand your repertoire to incorporate more complex multihit combos known as signature attacks. Use short, precise movements with the Wii Remote to execute Ahsoka's Shii-Cho Slash attack against Anakin.

**NOTE**

Shii-Cho Slash is Ahsoka's signature attack. To learn every duelist's signature attack, check the "Combos" section of a combatant's profile.

## Force Combos

The next step in your training is learning Force combos. Like the shorter, slightly less potent Composed combos, you can execute quick combination 'saber strikes imbued with the power of the Force! Unlike the other Force-imbued 'saber strikes, these Force combos require that your Force gauge be full. Once it is, activate the Force, then attack your opponent with a short two-hit combo.

The result is a quick, Force-powered combo that breaks your enemy's defenses, spins them around, and dishes out an extra bit of damage with a second blow. Because the Force gauge is full, the damage inflicted will increase!

# Lightsaber Clashes

## Lightsaber Lock 1

As Anakin explains, duelists often engage in lightsaber locks. When they do, the struggle to gain the advantage begins. During a Lightsaber Lock, both combatants will stand toe-to-toe with their 'sabers crossed. Engage Anakin in the Lightsaber Lock and wait for the timer to count down. When it does, shake the Wii Remote from left to right to break free of the lock!

Once free from the lock, you can quickly seize the moment and attack while your opponent is recovering.

they appear. You'll slowly fill the row of eight notches near your side of the screen. If you fill the eight notches before the enemy, your final blow will break the lock and fling your foe across the arena!

## Lightsaber Lock 3

The third type of Lightsaber Lock tests your ability to concentrate and react. During the lock, your opponent will try to anticipate your next move. As they do, you'll exchange tense

glances as both you and your enemy try to gain a mental advantage. Just as your foe is about to react, an onscreen prompt will appear. Immediately follow this to beat your rival to the slash, so to speak, and gain the advantage.

## Lightsaber Lock 2

While you are engaged in the second type of Lightsaber Lock, your opponent won't stand by idly and wait until the timer runs out. Instead, your rival will attempt to distract you by performing a series of moves. The only way to successfully emerge from this lock is to match the enemy move for move and eventually beat your opponent to the next move.

Watch the onscreen prompts as they appear at the screen's bottom, just below your position, and immediately execute them as

# Advanced Training
## Parrying

Parrying, like blocking and dodging, can be an underappreciated and underutilized aspect of combat. Against stronger opponents, it will not suffice to simply block incoming attacks. Eventually, your enemy will break your defences and launch a devastating attack. Instead of just blocking attacks, learn to parry and counterattack.

Follow Anakin's instructions to parry an attack, and counterattack immediately after. Above all other defensive measures, practice this technique the most. Some enemies in Campaign mode, Challenge mode, or Battle mode can be more easily bested with a fine balance of offense and defense. That includes parrying.

# Force Blast

Your final lesson aboard the Resolute is one of the Jedi's most useful abilities, the Force Blast. By harnessing the Force, concentrating it at a focal point, and quickly releasing it at a target, a Jedi can create a barely visible shock wave of energy. When it hits, the shock wave can knock over objects, fling foes far distances, and even break things! During battle, you can use Force Blast to knock enemies off balance and temporarily break their defense.

Follow Anakin's instructions and knock him over with a Force Blast attack. Once you've done this, your training on the Resolute is over. That doesn't mean that you won't continue to learn things about battle as you go. But for now, you've learned enough to continue on the adventure.

 **NOTE**

Anakin may have taught you how to handle your lightsaber and utilize the Force, but to see what you're really capable of, read the "Advanced Combat Techniques" chapter. Here you'll learn how to put everything you've learned together and formulate a fighting style. A Jedi never stops learning, even after he's become a Knight.

# TETH CASTLE DUNGEON

Treachery in the Outer Rim! As the Clone War rages across the galaxy, the Jedi Council learns that the son of Jabba the Hutt has been kidnapped. Sensing an opportunity to forge an alliance with the Hutt clan, Master Yoda sends Jedi Knight Anakin Skywalker and his Padawan, Ahsoka Tano, to the remote world of Teth, where they battle droid forces in an effort to rescue the Huttlet.

Little do the Jedi know that Count Dooku was behind the kidnapping, and the Separatist leader plans to frame the Jedi for the crime and sign his own treaty with Jabba. Dooku's sinister agent, Asajj Ventress, springs the trap, and Anakin finds himself surrounded and facing the deadly assassin....

## Anakin Skywalker vs. Asajj Ventress

VS.

| Force Attacks | Combos | Force Energy | Agility | Special |
|---|---|---|---|---|
| 4 | 3 | 3 | 3 | Force Blast |

| Force Attacks | Combos | Force Energy | Agility | Special |
|---|---|---|---|---|
| 3 | 3 | 3 | 4 | Exar Kun's Assault |

## Round 1

In your first battle, you face Asajj Ventress as Anakin Skywalker. Asajj can dual-wield, and her speed and agility make her a difficult duelist to contend with. When facing her in the first phase of battle, stay on the move and block consistently. Maintain a defensive posture against the speedier, more aggressive Ventress and wait for her to open up before launching an assault.

Ventress's dual-sword attacks make it difficult to anticipate her swing and make it difficult to parry accordingly; therefore, don't try to parry all of her attacks. Instead, block the majority of her advances and parry her noncombo strikes. However, that doesn't mean that you cannot parry her combos. If you miss her first strike, anticipate the second swing and parry the second blow in her multihit combo.

Her most powerful and dangerous attack is Exar Kun's Assault. With it she swings her two 'sabers like a windmill and savagely strikes you down. Stay quick on your feet and away from the arena's edge. If she corners you against a wall and launches into her Exar Kun's Assault, you'll be bantha feed in no time. Dodge her windmill-like assault by rolling to the side or leaping out of her reach.

Luckily, your greatest strength against Ventress are your Force attacks. Use the small pieces of debris scattered about to hurl them at the bald baddie and knock her off balance. As soon as she's off kilter, rush in and launch an assault. Spin her around with a Force-imbued attack, then strike her down with Tail of the Dragon or Determined Assault combos.

### HEALTH TRIGGERED EVENT

If you're reduced to 75 percent health, super battle droids enter the fray through the rear grate. If Asajj Ventress is reduced to 75 percent health, clones enter the fray through the rear grate. These events are mutually exclusive—if one is triggered the other will not.

### CAUTION

The stormtroopers in the castle may be on your side, but that doesn't mean that their blaster fire can't hurt you. Don't wander into their cross fire or you'll only help Ventress whittle down your health even faster!

After you beat Ventress once, she slowly begins to retreat deeper into Teth Castle. The battle rages on as you follow her down the castle steps into a dark and dank corridor. There, Ventress can't fend off your attack any longer, and you toss her against a weakened metal grate on the floor.

With a single 'saber strike, you slice through the grating, sending Ventress into a dark cavern deep inside the bowels of Teth Castle. Suddenly, a pair of blaster droids rushes out of a castle corridor and opens fire. With no choice but to escape, you leap into the cavern after the vulnerable Ventress.

### NOTE

No matter who emerges victorious in the first phase of battle, the second phase will take place in the castle caverns.

## Round 2

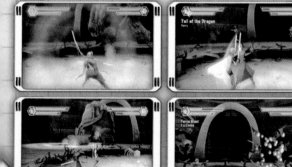

After besting Ventress once, the intensity increases in the second battle. The hairless harpy doesn't lose any of her agility or skills in the second match, so she's just as dangerous as she was before. Don't let your guard down! Instead, increase the amount of parrying attacks and maintain your defensive posture throughout the battle. Many of Ventress's attacks will remain the same, so nothing should surprise you by now.

Use the wide-open area in front of the large rancor beast to your advantage. Maneuver Ventress around the room toward objects you can use as projectiles. Use short stabbing strikes and Force Blast attacks to force Ventress where you want her to go. If she resists your attempts to steer her, wait for your Force meter to refill while you block, and resume your attack with short two- and three-hit combos.

After whittling down her health to less than half, start incorporating more Force-imbued attacks. Break her defenses and spin her around. Don't overuse your signature attacks, however. If you miss with the first blow of a signature attack, Ventress will use her speed and agility to capitalize and counterattack with her Exar Kun's Assault or Dark Acolyte Strike.

Once she is near defeat, increase the intensity of your attacks. Use more Force-imbued assaults or launch a Force Combo to bust through her defense and dish out Death Star–sized damage.

### HEALTH TRIGGERED EVENT

If your health is reduced to 90 percent, battle droids emerge to fight the rancor. If Ventress is reduced to 90 percent health, then clones emerge to battle the rancor. These events are mutually exclusive—if one is triggered, the other will not.

Even Ventress's second defeat isn't enough to smack some sense into the Sith assassin. You drive the defeated Ventress back, furiously striking at her with your 'saber, when suddenly, Dooku's puppet leaps back and retreats. She slides back, away from the reach of your lightsaber but directly into the path of the ornery rancor!

The beast slaps Ventress away into a dark corner of the castle. Now, even if you wanted to finish the fight once and for all, the rancor stands between you and your prey. Ventress may have gotten away for now, but she's not out of the woods yet.

# TETH CASTLE RAMPARTS

Caught in a Separatist trap! Anakin Skywalker and Ahsoka Tano have freed Jabba the Hutt's son from the dungeons of Teth Castle and eluded Count Dooku's assassin, Asajj Ventress. But the fortress is still overrun by the droid army.

Jedi Knight Obi-Wan Kenobi arrives just in time with Republic reinforcements and helps turn the tide of battle. While Anakin and Ahsoka try to escape with the Huttlet aboard the freighter Twilight, Obi-Wan confronts the Sith assassin....

# Obi-Wan Kenobi vs. Asajj Ventress

 VS.

| Force Attacks | Combos | Force Energy | Agility | Special |
|---|---|---|---|---|
| 2 | 5 | 4 | 3 | Force Blast |

| Force Attacks | Combos | Force Energy | Agility | Special |
|---|---|---|---|---|
| 3 | 3 | 3 | 4 | Exar Kun's Assault |

# Round 1

As expected, Ventress is not done fighting. This time, though, she must face you as Obi-Wan Kenobi. Because Obi-Wan is Anakin's master, their fighting styles can seem very similar at first glance. Anakin is a lot more reckless than Obi-Wan, so his combos aren't as effective, because Obi-Wan has practiced and perfected his combos over time. Use this to your advantage against Ventress during your first encounter.

Use short, quick two-hit combos to weaken Dooku's spy, then pounce on her when she least expects it and unleash Strength of Soresu attacks. Ventress may be a fiery creature, but she's no fool. She'll carefully stalk you as she slowly circles the arena with her guard raised. If you make one foolish move and expose yourself, she'll counter with her windmill-like attack and quickly make your regret your misstep.

Wait for her to move in as she circles. If you make the first move while her guard is raised, you'll pay for it more often than not. By letting her make the first move, you can deflect or parry her attack and follow up with a combo.

During the battle, the rear wall will explode and expose a fierce firefight between Dooku's forces and your stormtroopers. As you fight, slowly maneuver Ventress toward the opening and into the stray explosive blaster fire. Keep away from the opening as you move her into position to avoid taking any blaster fire. Capitalize on all successful Lightsaber Locks by immediately rushing the fallen Ventress and executing your signature attacks. With your combo skills and patience, Ventress is overmatched and will soon fall.

### HEALTH TRIGGERED EVENT

When either fighter is reduced to 75 percent health, the door at the back of the arena opens and a battle takes place between clones and droids.

### CAUTION

Watch out for the explosive blaster fire. If you take a hit, you'll take a great deal of damage and be knocked down, leaving you temporarily defenseless!

Once again, Ventress realizes she's on the brink of defeat, yet she continues to fight. Even though you Force slam her against the castle walls, she remains defiant. Realizing that this must end once and for all, you rush in for the attack, but Ventress blocks and deflects your blow! As you stagger back, the dark assassin leaps high into the air and retreats.

She escapes through one of the castle walls, but she doesn't get far. Just on the wall's other side is the castle rampart. You follow the vile creature to the rampart walkway, where you once again draw your sword...

## Round 2

The second phase of battle takes place in a far more constricted fighting space. The rampart walkway is slightly more narrow than the castle interior, so up and down movement is slightly restricted. Left and right movement, however, is unaffected. Use this to your advantage by forcing Ventress against the walkway walls and cornering her with strong combos and signature attacks. Her only escape

will be to leap over you. She will attempt to pounce on you from behind, but knowing this gives you the advantage. If she leaps into the air, either leap away before she can slash you from behind or attempt to intercept her before she strikes.

Continue to pummel Ventress with short combos and drive her back. If you allow her freedom about the walkway, she'll use her agility to spin around you and attack you from all angles. Take away her greatest asset—agility—by making her fight on your terms. Keep her off balance and consistently on the defensive. Don't attack wildly, but be consistent and calculating in your assaults.

As the walkway begins to crumble, use the resulting debris as projectiles. If she moves out of your 'saber's range, reach her with a well-thrown piece of concrete. As she staggers from the blow, move into range again and resume the assault.

Once she's near defeat, turn up the heat and attack with mainly Force Combos. Again, don't do this wildly and leave yourself open to counterattack, but do keep her pinned against the wall and spin her around so that you can launch a final combo while she's defenseless.

### HEALTH TRIGGERED EVENT

If either player is reduced to 90 percent health, a vulture droid will come screaming out of nowhere and crash into the bridge. It smashes a large section of the bridge into the abyss.

If you are reduced to 75 percent health, the Twilight will fly past in the background under fire from a horde of vulture droids. If Ventress is reduced to 75 percent health, the Twilight will fly past, attacking several vulture droids. Eventually it will zoom past the arena and release a big pile of crates from its cargo hold, destroying the pursuing vulture droids. When either fighter is reduced to 50 percent health, a mighty Venator will pass over the arena.

Finally, after her second defeat at your hands, Ventress musters the strength for one more assault. She swings her two 'sabers at you, attempting to break through your guard, but your defense is too strong. Her blows glance off your lightsaber with nothing but a mere flash of light. You turn the tables on her and slowly drive her back toward the broken part of the walkway. With one swift blast of the Force, you send Ventress across the broken walkway to the rampart's other side.

As she hits the rampart wall, the bricks behind her begin to crumble. Using the Force, you begin to pull on the wall to bring it down on top of Ventress. Just as the walls crumble over her, she leaps backward into a niche in the rampart. With the rubble in the way, there's no way to go after her! She makes one thing clear as she escapes, though: "Nothing is over."

# TATOOINE DUNE SEA

A race against time! Anakin Skywalker and Ahsoka Tano have rescued Jabba the Hutt's son from the droid army and escaped the ferocious Separatist blockade with the help of Obi-Wan Kenobi.

Eager to establish a treaty with the powerful Hutt clan, the Jedi speed across the galaxy to return the Huttlet to Jabba on Tatooine. But the evil Count Dooku will stop at nothing to foil the alliance.

He ambushes Skywalker in the desert, with plans to kill Jabba's son and blame Anakin for the foul deed....

## Anakin Skywalker vs. Count Dooku

VS.

| Force Attacks | Combos | Force Energy | Agility | Special |
|---|---|---|---|---|
| 4 | 3 | 3 | 3 | Force Blast |

| Force Attacks | Combos | Force Energy | Agility | Special |
|---|---|---|---|---|
| 2 | 5 | 5 | 2 | Sith Lightning |

## Round 1

The count is a calm, cold, and calculating creep, as evidenced by his many fiendish plans to destroy the Jedi. His fighting style reflects his calculating ways. When the fight against Dooku begins, the count will maintain a strict defensive position and will coolly walk around the area with his lightsaber in blocking position. Like Ventress, he'll often wait for you to make the first move and create an opening to exploit.

The difference between the count and Ventress, however, is that the count is a far more patient duelist. He can deflect the majority of your advances before striking, whereas Ventress would attack at the first hint of an opening. Turn Dooku's patience against him. Attack the traitorous Sith with short combos, letting him deflect the majority, and slowly knock him back. Slowly increase the intensity of your attacks until you can knock him off balance and create an opening for a stronger signature attack.

As you engage Count Dooku, keep your lightsaber raised to block his assaults. If he attacks with his special Sith Lightning ability, your 'saber will absorb it. Use well-timed evasive rolls to dodge Dooku's strikes, then immediately counterattack.

Dooku is far too powerful to frequently use your Force Blast. Instead of using it to knock him off balance, use it after hitting him with a thrown object. This will stun him long enough for you to formulate a more powerful assault. Use stabbing strikes to break through the count's defenses after knocking him back, and follow it up with signature attacks.

### HEALTH TRIGGERED EVENT

If you're reduced to 50 percent health, a series of vulture droids will perform a flyby from the arena's right side, and a gunship will crash into the background ruins on the level's left side.

If you reduce your opponent to 35 percent health, three gunships in the background will fly over the arena and fire missiles.

### CAUTION

Stay away from the sandstorms in the battle arena. If you get swallowed up by the sand, you'll take damage and be thrown off balance!

Dooku fell to your blade, but only for a moment. He immediately gets up and continues to fight. You drive him back with angry swings of your 'saber, and Count Dooku finally drops his veneer of composure and self-righteousness. Instead of relying simply on his "superior" abilities, he resorts to Sith-like treachery.

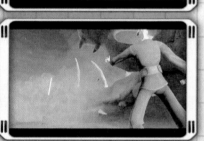

Just as you're about to run your 'saber through him, Dooku uses the Force to create a blinding sandstorm. The sand swallows you like a Sarlacc, and Dooku seizes the opportunity and runs away. You break through the sandstorm and give chase, catching the cowering count near the crumbling ruins by a Sarlacc pit.

## Round 2

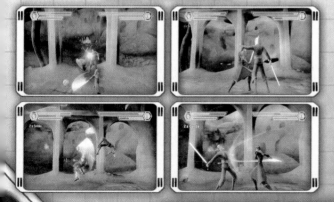

The second time around, Dooku is slightly more aggressive. He'll leap over your attacks, counterattack, and quickly launch devastating assaults. Stay on guard and match the count move for move. If he leaps over you to attack, leap away, then rush in. If he parries a blow, parry his counter. If the count hurls object at you, block and then throw objects at him.

Because Dooku is more aggressive, you can increase the intensity of your attacks during this phase. String together long signature attacks like Dune Sea Storm and Focused Offense, and use the shorter, two- or three-hit combos to keep the pressure on. The majority of the damage you'll inflict will come from signature attacks, not the smaller combos.

As you attack, stay away from Dooku's droids near the arena's edge, and fill up your Force Gauge. Once it's full, use it to slash through Dooku with a Force Combo and follow it up with strong signature attacks.

Capitalize on all Lightsaber Locks. Use these as you would defense-breaking attacks. After winning a Lightsaber Lock, rush the fallen fiend and continue your assault. Show Dooku that you cannot be bullied! Stay aggressive, maintain pressure, and keep the count off balance, and the battle will soon be over.

### HEALTH TRIGGERED EVENT

If you're reduced to 75 percent health, a gunship will crash in the background, center stage. If you're reduced to 55 percent health, two vulture droids will do flybys.

If the enemy is reduced to 80 percent health, a vulture droid will crash into the background on the left-hand side, killing several battle droids. If your rival is reduced to 55 percent health, a gunship will repeatedly descend into the background, fire at some battle droids, and then exit. Also, a vulture droid will perform a flyby from left to right.

This time, Count Dooku falls and fails to recover quickly. You swat him away with a single swipe and send the Sith soaring across the sandy dunes of Tatooine. He stands up defiantly and attacks, but you sidestep his feeble assault and surprise him with a Force Blast attack.

The force of your attack sends Dooku flying once again. This time, he falls helplessly into the mouth of the nearby Sarlacc. Still, something tells you that Dooku's not done.

# SEPARATIST LISTENING POST

A hero in enemy hands! Feared lost in battle, R2-D2 has been captured by the evil General Grievous. But the feisty astromech droid manages to send a signal that leads the Jedi to a secret Separatist listening post.

A Republic strike team infiltrates the station, and Anakin Skywalker attempts to rescue R2 before his data banks are compromised. While their clone troops complete the sabotage mission, Padawan Ahsoka Tano distracts General Grievous by engaging him in battle....

## Ahsoka Tano vs. General Grievous

VS.

| Force Attacks | Combos | Force Energy | Agility | Special |
| --- | --- | --- | --- | --- |
| 2 | 1 | 2 | 5 | Force Blast |

| Force Attacks | Combos | Force Energy | Agility | Special |
| --- | --- | --- | --- | --- |
| 5 | 3 | 0 | 1 | Saber Onslaught |

## Round 1

General Grievous may have the upper hand when it comes to Force attacks and combos, but you've got two very important things that he lacks: Force Energy and a high Agility rating. Both of these swing the scales in your favor. The Listening Post arena may not seem smaller than other battle arenas, but the environmental hazards shrink the fighting area substantially. Scattered around the arena are small breaches in the electrical conduits. Use these to short-circuit the general and inflict damage while you fight.

Use your speed and agility to dodge Grievous's attacks and counter with quick combos and signature attacks. If Grievous attacks with short combos and swift strikes, block his assault, then immediately launch into a flurry of combos. The best way to keep Grievous off balance is to overwhelm him with a constant stream of 'saber strikes and combos.

Follow Grievous around the arena, striking, slashing, and stabbing as you go, and keep heavy pressure on him. If he retaliates, back far enough away to get out of his range, then resume your attack. Grievous's four 'sabers make it difficult to feel out his attacks, so don't try to parry his blows unless you're certain you know where they're coming from. Otherwise, stay on the move and dodge!

After building up a Force charge and filling your Force Gauge, use Force-imbued strikes and Force combos to finish off the pile of nuts and bolts.

## HEALTH TRIGGERED EVENT

# Round 2

Each of the following events will only play once. It will not trigger until the previous event has played out, so if you finish the first event quickly, you might miss out on seeing all the events.

When either player is reduced to 90 percent health, the gunship parked on the level's left side takes some laser fire and explodes. If either player is reduced to 80 percent health, a gunship will fly in and land on the right platform and drop off four clones that will run to the main background platform and start firing on the droids in the distance.

If either player gets reduced to 70 percent health, a vulture droid careers out of control from the level's left side and collides with the large radar dish on the skystation, causing the dish to detach and pass over the arena, dropping debris. When either player is reduced to 60 percent health, the gunships carrying droids in the background will explode and fall out of sight, but not before firing several missiles that eliminate all the droids.

If either player gets reduced to 50 percent health, the Twilight takes off and R2-D2 and Goldie come down to the platform behind you and begin fighting. If either player gets reduced to 40 percent health, Yoda and some clones will do a quick flyby at the front of the arena.

General Grievous is just as hot-tempered and stubborn as the other Sith puppets. Unfortunately, he only becomes more agitated after falling to a Padawan in the first fight and comes out swinging in the second fight. Raise your lightsaber to block his Great Jedi Purge attacks, and move out of his reach. Grievous will continue to attack and move forward; as he does, roll to the side and attack from his rear or his sides.

Stalk the general around the arena and slash at him with your combo flurries. Maintain the same pressure on Grievous as in the first fight, but block more and stay on the move. As Grievous approaches, speed away from him and find an opening to exploit.

If Grievous attempts to rush you with his Saber Storm attack, leap away and block. Don't attempt to parry or counter-attack; instead simply wait for Grievous to back away again. When he does, rush the metallic monster and mince him with signature attacks.

Once General Grievous is near defeat, begin using more Force combos and Force-imbued attacks. Spin the general around and attack him from behind. Eventually, Dooku's pet android will fall to your 'saber.

Much to Grievous's surprise, you bested him in battle! But like Ventress and Dooku before him, he's fighting for the Sith and won't give up easily. He takes a moment to gather his strength and quickly recovers.

Suddenly, without warning, the general turns from a huddled pile of parts on the ground to a spiderlike machine crawling on all fours. Then he's back up on two feet with four lightsabers active and thirsting for Padawan blood. This fight it not over yet.

 NOTE

There are no Health Triggered Events during the second phase of battle.

 NOTE

This battle does not change locations for the second phase.

Grievous's strength is useless against you. After all, he can't hurt what he can't catch! After falling a second time to your blade, Grievous is even more upset. He leaps to his feet and spins all four blades at you, hoping to slice you to ribbons, but you deftly evade his attacks and slide past him underneath his legs.

You stand up immediately and turn around. Your 'saber bites into the general's back, angering him even more. He spins around and swings his blades one more time, hoping to catch you with them, but you're too fast. The Listening Post begins to crumble around him, and you see an opportunity. The general has tasted defeat at the hands of a Padawan, and your mission to distract him is a success. A dropship swings by and you hop on as Grievous is pummeled by the crumbling Listening Post.

**LIGHTSABER DUELS**

PRIMA OFFICIAL GAME GUIDE

# THE TRANQUILITY

A Separatist leader is captured! Nute Gunray's plan to entrap Senator Padmé Amidala backfires, and the devious Trade Federation viceroy finds himself in the custody of Republic forces.

Fearing that the cowardly Neimoidian will reveal their secrets to the Jedi, Darth Sidious and Count Dooku dispatch Asajj Ventress to infiltrate the Republic warship carrying Gunray to Coruscant and rescue him before he can betray them. Only Padawan Ahsoka Tano stands between Ventress and her prize....

# Ahsoka Tano vs. Asajj Ventress

 **VS.**

| Force Attacks | Combos | Force Energy | Agility | Special |
|---|---|---|---|---|
| 2 | 1 | 2 | 5 | Force Blast |

| Force Attacks | Combos | Force Energy | Agility | Special |
|---|---|---|---|---|
| 3 | 3 | 3 | 4 | Exar Kun's Assault |

# Round 1

Even though you have the Agility advantage, Ventress's other skills make this a difficult fight. You can't just overwhelm her with combos and speed like you could Grievous. The fight against Ventress takes a lot more patience, defense, and planning. As you fight aboard the Tranquility, the room explodes around you. Keep the fight near the arena's edges and maintain a strong defense as you move.

Block Ventress's attacks, then counter. Even if she blocks your attacks, force her to move toward the small explosives scattered along the room's edge. If she escapes your attacks and leaps away, rush toward her and catch her as she lands and prepares to attack you. If you leave her unchecked, Ventress can quickly launch several multihit combos and slice off a big chunk from your Health meter!

Follow Ventress as she creeps around the arena, and occasionally hit her with quick combos. Pursue her until you can pin her against the wall. Once she's pinned, unleash several combos like Strength of the Sarlacc and Sun Djem Strike.

After bringing Ventress to less than 50 percent, back away and wait for her to come at you. Deflect her attacks and counter. Strike at her just enough to fill your Force meter, then let loose on her with Force combos.

When either combatant is reduced to 95 percent health, the rear doors explode, revealing clone troopers and super battle droids fighting in the background. When either fighter is reduced to 70 percent health, detonators on the ground start to explode, one after another.

If you're reduced to 80 percent health, the super battle droids in the left corridor start firing into the main arena. If your health is reduced to 75 percent, the super battle droids in the right corridor start firing into the main arena. If you're reduced to 15 percent health, explosions occur in the central corridor, decimating the clone troopers, and battle droids run in.

Ventress falls to her knees but quickly regains her composure. Rather than take the loss to a Padawan, Ventress shoves you away and begins to head toward a hole in the wall. You follow her, slashing at her as you go, but she blocks your attacks and continues to inch toward her escape. As you follow, she takes one dangerous swing at your head, but you bend at the last minute and avoid certain death.

Suddenly, an explosion rocks the Tranquility, and Asajj seizes the opportunity. She motions toward the hole in the wall and quickly leaps out. She thinks she's escaped, but she hasn't. You follow hot on her heels!

## Round 2

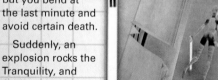

The second phase of battle takes place on a crumbling section of the Tranquility. Fires rage, thrusters ignite, and explosions erupt around you as you take on Ventress. Watch out for flying debris, as there are a lot more loose objects that Ventress can use as projectiles. Beat her to the punch and use the scrap metal against her before she can hurl it at you.

Leap over Ventress as she approaches and attack her from behind. This knocks her off her feet and leaves her vulnerable to a follow-up signature attack. Ventress will attempt to string together very short combos, then move away. If she lands a two-hit assault, she'll end it with a second attack or a longer combo before backing away and doing it again.

If she gets into a rhythm, don't try to counterattack. Instead, block the first attack in her short flurry, then back away so that her second assault cannot hit. By doing so, you remove any chance of her building momentum and allow yourself time to formulate your own attack.

Stay on the move, blocking and dodging until Ventress gives you an opening. When she does, lash out at her with three-hit combos to whittle down her health. Finish off Dooku's bald bully with strong signature attacks and Force combos.

Once either fighter is reduced to 95 percent health, debris begins falling in the background.

 **CAUTION**

At the arena's edge, watch for the thrusters to ignite and the large boosters on the right to turn red-hot. When they do, they'll ignite and fire across the entire arena! Stay out of the way and leap onto the raised area to dodge the booster fire.

After falling a second time to your skills, Ventress is white-hot mad! She attacks and you defend. You use your agility to deftly dodge her attacks. When two broken thrusters appear on the ground, you see an opportunity and take it.

You hurl the thrusters at her, but she dodges and slices past them. In a final effort, you Force Blast her back into a primed booster. She slams against the booster just as it fires! Ventress is consumed by the blast, but is she finished for good?

# THE NEGOTIATOR

Terror spreads across the galaxy! Under the command of General Grievous, a powerful new Separatist battleship, the Malevolence, has destroyed dozens of Republic vessels in a string of ruthless surprise attacks.

Anakin Skywalker leads a daring bombing mission against the warship, while Obi-Wan Kenobi races to defend a vital clone medical station. But the evil Count Dooku ambushes Obi-Wan's fleet and boards his command ship, determined to slay the heroic Jedi Knight....

## Obi-Wan Kenobi vs. Count Dooku

 VS.

| Force Attacks | Combos | Force Energy | Agility | Special |
|---|---|---|---|---|
| 2 | 5 | 4 | 3 | Force Blast |

| Force Attacks | Combos | Force Energy | Agility | Special |
|---|---|---|---|---|
| 2 | 5 | 5 | 2 | Sith Lightning |

## Round 1

The battle between Obi-Wan and Count Dooku is far more balanced than other encounters with Dooku. Because the two duelists are well versed in the ways of the Force and in lightsaber combat, their Force attacks and combo abilities are well matched. The battle arena is of average size, but the myriad of computer consoles and displays make it a difficult area in which to battle. The key to victory is to effectively use your combos in this restricted battle arena.

Count Dooku will begin by playing it safe, as always. He'll carefully edge to the sides of the battle arena with his lightsaber raised and ready to block. If you attack, he'll either deflect your attacks or leap over you and attack from behind. Approach Dooku with your 'saber raised to block, and attack with strong combos. Use your stabbing attack to break through his defense and follow it up with a signature attack.

If Count Dooku leaps over you, immediately turn around and attack him as he lands. You've got a slight advantage over him with Agility, so you're a bit faster. Follow Dooku around the arena and pummel him as he attempts to maneuver around the many obstacles. Use the environment to your advantage and force Count Dooku to contend with you and the consoles, displays, and other things in his way.

If the computer consoles are difficult for you to maneuver around as well, lure Dooku to the room's left side and destroy the consoles there. This will create a large wide-open area where you can safely engage in battle without hindrance. Use the crates scattered about the area as projectiles against Dooku before he can hurl them at you.

Parry Dooku's attacks and counterattack consistently. Occasionally use Force Blast to knock the count off his guard, then rush in with a stabbing attack. As he staggers, launch your combo and signature attacks to deal major damage. If he parries your advances, back away and lure him toward you to create an opening.

### HEALTH TRIGGERED EVENT

**Once either combatant is reduced to 90 percent health, the doors explode, revealing a fierce battle between clone troopers and super battle droids in the background. Super battle droid plasma bolts begin flying into the battle arena.**

After knocking Dooku to his knees, the stubborn count gets back to his feet immediately. You lock swords and exchange heated words with the traitor! Your swords break only to meet a second, third, and fourth time. You shove Dooku back with a Force Blast but he resists. Just as he is about to counterattack, you anticipate his blow and knock him into the next room.

In the next room, your allied stormtroopers attack Dooku. He quickly dispatches them with his Sith Lightning attacks, but the stormtroopers slow him down just long enough for you to speed past two shutting hatch doors. The hatch slams shut behind you, leaving you and Dooku all alone in the large circular room.

# Round 2

The second phase of battle occurs inside a large circular room with a thin walkway running down the room's center. Though the room is large, the area on which you can fight is small and oddly shaped, making long signature attack chains and combo strings difficult to achieve. The lack of debris and equipment in the room's center also make this a perfect arena for the purest form of battle—'saber versus 'saber.

Lure Dooku to the near end of the center walkway. There you can use the long walkway ahead and the areas to its left and right to your advantage. By keeping Dooku in this area, you can maximize your combos and signature attacks without having to restrict your movement. The area is still tight and will keep you in closer quarters than other arenas, so keep your 'saber consistently raised to block.

If the battle spills into the room's long curved edges, lure Dooku back toward the center. Build up your Force charge and unleash a Force Combo as soon as your Force Gauge is full. Spin Dooku around and lash out at him with more combos.

After depleting nearly 90 percent of his health, dive Dooku back against a wall and pin him with several savage 'saber strikes. Use Force-imbued attacks and finish off the Sith Lord.

## HEALTH TRIGGERED EVENT

The Malevolence will arrive based on which of the following two events is triggered first. If your health is reduced to 90 percent, Separatist frigates come out of hyperspace and begin firing on the Republic forces. After a little while, the Malevolence will come out of hyperspace to join the fray.

If Count Dooku's health is reduced to 90 percent, Republic Venators come out of hyperspace and begin firing on the Separatist forces. The Malevolence will soon come out of hyperspace to join the fray. After a short delay, a phalanx of Y-wing, accompanied by Anakin and Plo Koon's starfighters, roar past to attack the Malevolence.

If you are reduced to 65 percent health, several vulture droids attack the bridge of Obi-Wan's Venator, cracking the glass. One of the Republic Venators begins to explode and drift from view. If Dooku is reduced to 65 percent health, several torrents and vulture droids begin fighting in between the spacecraft, and one of the Separatist frigates explodes and drifts from view.

If you are reduced to 50 percent health , several torrents and vulture droids begin fighting in between the spacecraft. The second Republic Venator will explode and sink from view. After both Venators have been destroyed, the Malevolence begins firing at the bridge of Obi-Wan's Venator, causing it to shudder with explosions and arc electricity. If Dooku is reduced to 50 percent health, several torrents and vulture droids begin fighting in between the spacecraft. The second Separatist frigate will begin to explode and sink from view.

Dooku gets off his feet a second time and rushes at you with his lightsaber swinging. You defend against his attacks and fling your feeble foe against the ship's window with a Force Blast. Dooku lands on his knees and is weakened by the impact against the window. Just then, your stormtroopers arrive and prepare to arrest Dooku. You've won and captured the savage Sith Lord!

Before you can secure him, however, Anakin contacts you, in need of help. With no choice but to help your former Padawan, you leave Dooku in the hands of your stormtroopers. Dooku, confident that the small battalion of troopers won't be enough to subdue him, smirks as you flee.

# THE MALEVOLENCE

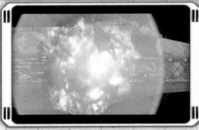

A Senator in danger! Anakin Skywalker's fearless Gold Squadron damages the Malevolence, but the Republic fleet does not have enough power to finish the job.

To cover his retreat, General Grievous takes Senator Padmé Amidala hostage. Before the Malevolence can escape, Anakin and his Padawan slip aboard to rescue the Senator and sabotage the mighty warship, while Obi-Wan Kenobi faces off against the bloodthirsty droid general....

## Obi-Wan Kenobi vs. General Grievous

# VS.

| Force Attacks | Combos | Force Energy | Agility | Special |
|---|---|---|---|---|
| 2 | 5 | 4 | 3 | Force Blast |

| Force Attacks | Combos | Force Energy | Agility | Special |
|---|---|---|---|---|
| 5 | 3 | 0 | 1 | Saber Onslaught |

## Round 1

The battle against Grievous takes place atop a transport system inside the Malevolence. Because the transport tram is so long, you lose a bit of upward and downward movement in the arena; however, you gain a lot of left and right movement. This arena is perfect for stringing together long chains of combos and signature attacks.

Keep the battle in your favor by fighting very technically. Use a healthy dose of Force Blasts to keep Grievous off kilter, and continuously pummel him with combos. You can't overwhelm him like Ahsoka would, so don't try. Instead, fight with a good balance of blocking, parrying, and dodging in between attacks. If the general attempts to hit you with his signature attacks, leap back and away to escape his reach, then rush in with a stabbing attack when he stops approaching.

If Grievous uses the little depth in this arena, execute leaping attacks to soar over the general and land with your 'saber running down his back. Not only does it inflict damage, but it also knocks him to his knees. Take advantage of all successful Lightsaber Locks and always follow up with combos and signature attacks.

Lead Grievous back and forth along the tram, dodging blaster bolts as you go. Don't chase Grievous; make him chase you and continuously ambush him with Ataru Surge and Eye of the Storm once he's below 25 percent health.

### CAUTION

Watch out for the droid blaster bolts that streak in from the distance. If they hit you, they'll explode and knock you off your feet! When you see the droid blaster bolt frequency start to ramp up, it's a good idea to advance to the next train car.

### NOTE

There are no Health Triggered Events in the first phase of battle.

Grievous falls but quickly rises to his feet. He's determined to beat you and doesn't bother fleeing to a second location. This fight started on the tram and will finish on the tram!

## Round 2

Expect Grievous to begin the second phase of battle more aggressively. He'll use attacks like Saber Onslaught and leaping slashes more often. Keep your guard up and slowly move away from him so that you're not always within striking distance. If you stay within striking distance, Grievous will pummel you, break your defense, and execute several strings of combos and signature attacks.

Instead, lure Grievous toward you and use the raised area at either end of the tram to create a barrier

between you and him. When he tries to leap over the barrier, ambush him with several strong 'saber strikes followed by short combos.

On the tram's far end, the battle arena shrinks to nearly one-fourth the size. If you're comfortable stringing together chains of two-and three-hit combos, use the area's tight space to pummel Grievous. Pin him against the area's right end, forcing him to either get through you to get back to the main tram or to leap down onto the smaller area on the far right. If he retreats farther to the right, follow him and land with a downward slash attack.

Once his health dips below 40 percent, take the fight back to the main tram. There you can use the tram's length to drive Grievous back with a combination of signature attacks and Force combos.

### HEALTH TRIGGERED EVENT

If Grievous is reduced to 50 percent health, you'll see Plo Koon in the background, chasing a group of vulture droids. If you're reduced to 50 percent health, you'll see Plo Koon in the background being chased by a group of vulture droids. These events are mutually exclusive—if one happens, the other will not.

Just when Grievous is about to fall to your blade, he musters up one final attack. He rushes you with all four lightsabers spinning but misses every attack! You leap into the air just before he can launch a second attack, and the tram explodes while you're in midair. As you land, Grievous begins to throw pieces of debris at you, but you swat the metal chunks away like they were Tatooine desert flies.

You shove the metal monster back with a Force Blast and connect with a 'saber strike. Just as you're about

to connect with a second attack, Grievous leaps onto a crate and raises a box high into the air. Before he can crush you, however, the tram speeds by a metal beam that slams him in the head and knocks the foolish fiend off the tram.

# SEPARATIST DROID LAB

A new threat! Clone intelligence has uncovered the existence of a dangerous new secret weapon being constructed aboard a mysterious Separatist laboratory.

Anakin Skywalker eludes the enemy starfleet and finds the lab hidden deep in the Outer Rim. Once inside, Anakin battles his way to the heart of the vessel, where he confronts the Jedi Council's darkest fears....

## Anakin Skywalker vs. EG-05 Jedi Hunter

VS.

| Force Attacks | Combos | Force Energy | Agility | Special |
|:---:|:---:|:---:|:---:|:---:|
| 4 | 3 | 3 | 3 | Force Blast |

| Force Attacks | Combos | Force Energy | Agility | Special |
|:---:|:---:|:---:|:---:|:---:|
| 4 | 3 | 0 | 3 | Dark Blast |

## Round 1

Like Ventress and Grievous, the Jedi hunter droid wields more than one lightsaber. That makes parrying its attacks more difficult than other warriors', but it's not impossible. Block the droid's advances and counterattack with Tail of the Dragon and Determined Assault attacks. Knock the droid back with your signature strikes, then back away before it can retaliate.

If it brings its hand up and begins to charge, either leap out of the way or rush it with a stabbing attack to stop it from scorching you with its Dark Blast attack. Maintain a balanced assault and keep from flailing wildly with long combos. If you miss, your momentum will keep you off balance and the killer droid will simply leap over you and slash you from behind.

Make full use of the crates and metal objects lying around. Throw them at the hunter droid in between attacks to keep the machine's servos spinning. If you keep the EG-05 constantly on the defensive, you'll always have the upper hand. If the droid manages to launch a successful attack, immediately back away to keep it from overwhelming you with combos.

Use Force Blast when backing away from an attack and knock the droid around from a distance, then rush it before it can sprint toward you and attack. Be aggressive but not foolish. After several exchanges, you'll deplete the droid's health to less than 30 percent. When you do, combine Force-imbued attacks with lots of leaping slashes to bring it down.

## HEALTH TRIGGERED EVENT

If either fighter is reduced to 50 percent health, the core begins to shake as it starts overloading, and reams of lightning begin streaming from the core and heading into the arena.

Like Grievous before it, the EG-05 Jedi hunter droid will not stay down. Defeat is not part of its programming. As soon as it falls to your blade, it leaps back up to its feet. With both swords blazing and ready to go, the Jedi hunter droid slowly creeps toward you.

## Round 2

During the second phase of battle, the arena becomes more and more unstable. Electrical currents run wildly at the far end, creating an environmental hazard. Use it to your advantage by slamming the machine into the wall.

Corner the Separatists' robot against the arena's edge, deliver a signature attack, then back away before it can leap over you and attack from behind. Force the Jedi hunter to the arena's rear end and corner it behind the large console at the room's center. Pick it apart with a few short combos, then retreat back to the main room.

There, reengage the droid and chip away at it even more. If it begins to leap about, chase after it. If you stand still while it leaps around the arena, it'll attack you from above and behind, so stay on the move and catch it while it lands!

After depleting its health to less than 30 percent, attack it just as you did before, with Force-imbued attacks and leaping attacks.

## HEALTH TRIGGERED EVENT

Once either fighter is reduced to 95 percent health, the lightning streaks into the arena at a faster rate. When either fighter's health is reduced to 60 percent, the core goes critical, tearing the level apart as it shakes its foundations. The lightning enters the arena even more quickly!

After depleting all of the droid's health, it somehow manages to regain a bit of power. It runs toward you with its 'sabers ready for action, but you thrust it back with a quick combo. The robot leaps into the air, avoiding your attack, then rushes toward you one more time. Just as it is about to slash through you, you block its attack and spin behind it.

Your first slash cuts through the droid's left arm. It reels back in surprise and you launch yourself at it, delivering a devastating kick. With no way to

defend itself, the robot staggers while you spin around one more time and circle behind it. Your blade flashes a brilliant white-blue as it cuts through the EG-05's servos and motors. Finally, after taking too much damage, the robot explodes into a shower of junk parts. The Jedi are safe from becoming prey...for now.

# SECRET JEDI SCROLLS

The following secret Jedi scrolls were found among the many ruins that remained after the Clone Wars. They detail information on how to unlock every fighter, costume, concept art gallery, and other unlockables in *Star Wars: The Clone Wars—Lightsaber Duels*.

| Character | Complete |
|---|---|
| Count Dooku | Campaign: Tatooine |
| General Grievous | Campaign: Separatist Listening Post |
| EG-05 Jedi Hunter Droid | Campaign: Separatist Droid Lab |
| Kit Fisto | Challenge mode: Complete 9 challenges |
| Mace Windu | Challenge mode: Complete 18 challenges |
| Plo Koon | Challenge mode: Complete 27 challenges |

| Challenge Modes | Complete |
|---|---|
| Anakin Skywalker's Challenge mode | Tutorial: Beginner |
| Asajj Ventress's Challenge mode | Tutorial: Beginner |
| Obi-Wan Kenobi's Challenge mode | Campaign: Teth Palace |
| Count Dooku's Challenge mode | Campaign: Tatooine |
| Ahsoka Tano's Challenge mode | Campaign: Separatist Listening Post |
| General Grievous's Challenge mode | Campaign: Separatist Listening Post |
| EG-05 Jedi hunter droid's Challenge mode | Campaign: Separatist Droid Lab |
| Kit Fisto's Challenge mode | Challenge mode: Complete 9 challenges |
| Mace Windu's Challenge mode | Challenge mode: Complete 18 challenges |
| Plo Koon's Challenge mode | Challenge mode: Complete 27 challenges |

| Cheats/Difficulty Mode | Complete |
|---|---|
| Epic Battle | Campaign: Teth Monastery |
| Danger Mode | Campaign: Teth Palace |
| Lightsaber Locks | Campaign: Tatooine |
| Lightsaber Only | Campaign: Separatist Listening Post |
| No Power | Campaign: The Tranquility |
| No Distractions | Campaign: The Negotiator |
| Risk | Campaign: The Malevolence |
| Full Power | Campaign: Separatist Droid Lab |
| Grand Master Difficulty | Complete Story mode |

| Videos | Complete |
|---|---|
| TR Intro | Campaign: Teth Monastery |
| TB Intro | Campaign: Teth Palace |
| TT Intro | Campaign: Tatooine |
| SS Intro | Campaign: Separatist Listening Post |
| JC Intro | Campaign: The Tranquility |
| VB Intro | Campaign: The Negotiator |
| ML Intro | Campaign: The Malevolence |
| SD Intro | Campaign: Separatist Droid Lab |
| Credits | Complete Story mode |

| Arena | Complete |
|---|---|
| Teth Monastery | Tutorial: Beginner |
| Droid Factory | Challenge mode: Complete 4 challenges |
| Raxus Prime | Challenge mode: Complete 13 challenges |
| Sarlacc Pit | Challenge mode: Complete 22 challenges |
| Mustafar | Challenge mode: Complete 32 challenges |

| Art Gallery | Complete |
|---|---|
| Early work | Challenge mode: Complete 9 challenges |
| Level design | Challenge mode: Complete 18 challenges |
| Character costumes concept art | Challenge mode: Complete 27 challenges |
| EG-05 Jedi hunter droid evolution art gallery | Challenge mode: Complete all 40 challenges |

| Alternate Costumes | Complete |
|---|---|
| All Jedi 3rd costumes | Challenge mode: Complete 32 challenges |
| All Sith 3rd costumes | Challenge mode: Complete 36 challenges |
| High Council 3rd costumes | Challenge mode: Complete all 40 challenges |
| Anakin Skywalker's Jedi Knight robes | Complete all four of Anakin Skywalker's challenges |
| Ahsoka Tano's Padawan robes | Complete all four of Ahsoka Tano's challenges |
| Obi-Wan Kenobi's ceremonial battle gear | Complete all four of Obi-Wan Kenobi's challenges |
| Asajj Ventress's acolyte robes | Complete all four of Asajj Ventress's challenges |
| General Grievous's Sith markings | Complete all four of General Grievous's challenges |
| Count Dooku Sith robes | Complete all four of Count Dooku's challenges |
| EG-4 prototype | Complete all four of the EG-05 Jedi hunter droid's challenges |
| Kit Fisto's Jedi Council robes | Complete all four of Kit Fisto's challenges |
| Mace Windu's Jedi Council robes | Complete all four of Mace Windu's challenges |
| Plo Koon's Jedi Council robes | Complete all four of Plo Koon's challenges |
| Anakin Skywalker's Tatooine battle gear | Complete Battle mode as Anakin Skywalker |
| Ahsoka Tano's training outfit | Complete Battle mode as Ahsoka Tano |
| Obi-Wan Kenobi's Kashyyyk battle gear | Complete Battle mode as Obi-Wan Kenobi |
| Asajj Ventress's assassin battle gear | Complete Battle mode as Asajj Ventress |
| General Grievous's Supreme General battle gear | Complete Battle mode as General Grievous |
| Count Dooku's Confederacy battle gear | Complete Battle mode as Count Dooku |
| EG-3 prototype | Complete Battle mode as EG-05 Jedi hunter droid |
| Kit Fisto's High General robe | Complete Battle mode as Kit Fisto |
| Mace Windu's Jedi Master robe | Complete Battle mode as Mace Windu |
| Plo Koon's Jedi robe | Complete Battle mode as Plo Koon |

**NOTE**

Enter the following cheats in the Cheats menu to unlock the desired content. When doing so, enter the button commands quickly for the cheat to work.

| Cheat | Unlocks |
|---|---|
| 22+22+22-A-C-Z+Z | Unlock Count Dooku |
| 22+22+22-Z-A-C+C | Unlock General Grievous |
| AZCCAZ+2 | Unlock Resolute Hangar |
| AAAZZZCCC+1 | Unlock Sarlacc Pit |
| ZZZZZ+ZZZZZ+1 | Unlock Mustafar |
| AAAAA+AAAAA+2 | Unlock Raxus Prime |
| CCCCC+CCCCC+1 | Unlock Separatist Droid Factory |
| A+22+C+22+Z+22 | Unlocks all Story Mode levels |
| -A+1 | Early Works concept art gallery |
| -A+2 | Level Design concept art gallery |
| +A+1+2 | Evolution of the Jedi Hunter Droid concept art gallery |
| +A+2+2 | Character Costumes concept art gallery |
| 12+1 | Unlocks Credits |

# CONCEPT ART

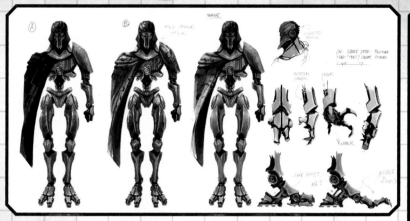

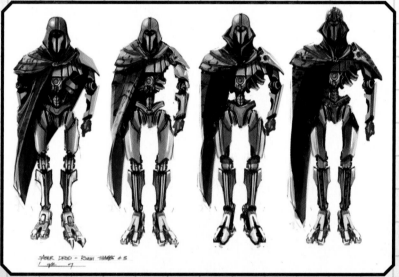

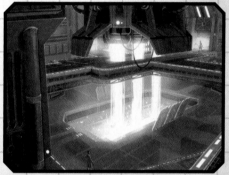

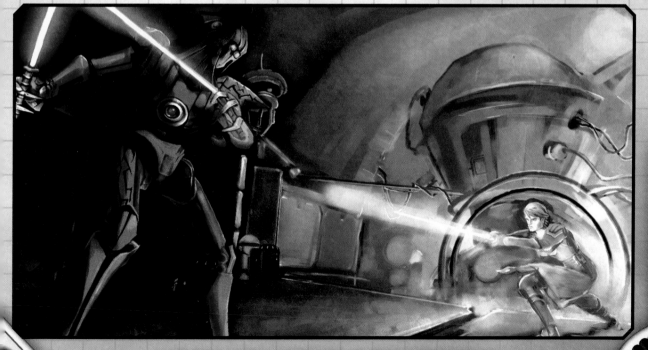

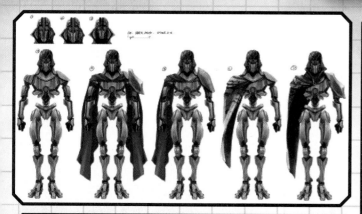

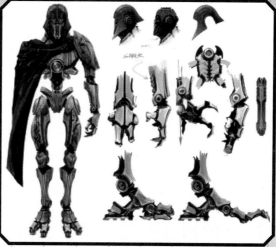

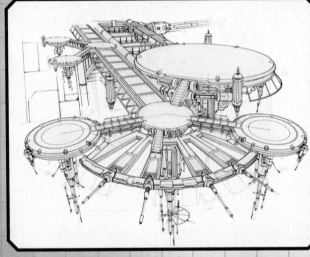

# STAR WARS
# THE CLONE WARS
## JEDI ALLIANCE™

### PRIMA OFFICIAL GAME GUIDE

**Written by:**
**Fernando Bueno**

**Prima Games**
An Imprint of Random House, Inc.
3000 Lava Ridge Court, Suite 100
Roseville, CA 95661
www.primagames.com

Senior Product Manager: Donato Tica
Associate Product Manager: John Browning
Manufacturing: Stephanie Sanchez
Design & Layout: Calibre Grafix

**Acknowledgements**
Vince Kudirka, Gavin Leung, Stephen Ervin, Rebecca Aghakhan-Mooshiabad, Cai Jiahui.

ISBN: 978-0-7615-6132-3
Library of Congress Catalog Card Number: 2008937618
Printed in the United States of America

08 09 10 11 LL 10 9 8 7 6 5 4 3 2 1

## CONTENTS

Fernando "Red Star" Bueno (aka dukkhah) has been a gamer since opening his first Atari, and has been writing creatively since his early years in high school. During college he combined his loves for gaming and writing and began freelancing for popular gaming websites. The San Diego native found his way to Northern California shortly after high school. After graduating from the University of California, Davis, with a dual degree in English and art history, he was able to land a job as an editor for Prima Games. Though happy with his position as an editor, his life called him to Las Vegas where he now resides. During the move to Nevada, he also made the move to author and has since written a number of game books, including *Naruto Uzumaki Chronicles 2*, *Prince of Persia: Two Thrones*, *Fight Night Round 3*, and *Stubbs the Zombie*.

In his time off he enjoys the works of Hermann Hesse, Johann Van Goethe, Franz Kafka, and EGM. When not writing for Prima, he continues to work on his craft as a poet.

We want to hear from you! E-mail comments and feedback to fbueno@primagames.com.

# THE CLONE WARS: JEDI ALLIANCE

## GAME OVERVIEW

The Clone Wars rage across the entire galaxy! The forces of the Republic, led by the valiant Jedi Knights, must defend against Count Dooku, General Grievous, and the Separatist Army.

When a cargo of precious lightsaber crystals is mysteriously hijacked, Anakin Skywalker and his new Padawan, Ahsoka Tano, are sent to recover it. What begins as a routine investigation leads to a test of will for the fearless Jedi. Anakin, Ahsoka, and eventually Jedi Masters Obi-Wan Kenobi, Mace Windu, Plo Kloon, and Kit Fisto must band together to face a terrifying new enemy. The Jedi must combine their individual powers in new ways to overcome a sinister force that can match their skills with the lightsaber and even the Force!

The future of the entire Republic is at stake…will our heroes prevail?

At the start of each mission, you choose two Jedi from a selection of six. The pairing of the Jedi gives you access to abilities that are unique to each Jedi team.

Using this combination of the Jedis' unique abilities, you battle through nine action-packed levels that feature innovative, stylus-based combat, unique environments, Jedi Master-level puzzles, and several different types of minigames!

JEDI ALLIANCE™
Touch the Touch Screen

## HOW TO USE THIS BOOK

### TIP

These Tip boxes are scattered around the pages of this book. Whenever you see one of these boxes, read the information contained within. Tip boxes provide tidbits of information that help you fight better, locate hidden items, and often enhance your experience.

### NOTE

Notes may not enhance your abilities or experience, but they will provide information on the game or the book. You can live without these, but if you thirst for knowledge, read them!

### CAUTION

If you ignore Tip or Note boxes, then definitely read Caution boxes. Other boxes may make you a better Jedi or a notch smarter, but only Caution boxes will keep you alive. The sole purpose of Caution boxes is to provide you vital warnings of dangers that may lay ahead.

### TRIVIA BOX

These sidebars are for true *Star Wars* fans. Each trivia box contains little bits of info on the *Jedi Alliance* plot, game, and the people who made it!

# THE CAST

## THE JEDI ORDER

The following section details all the playable characters in *Jedi Alliance*.

### Ahsoka Tano

#### Vitals

**Allegiance:** The Republic

**Rank:** Commander

**Class:** Padawan

**Species:** Togruta

**Height:** 1.61

**Force Power:** Environmental

## Combo Attacks

| Combo | 1st Hit | 2nd Hit | 3rd Hit | 4th Hit |
|---|---|---|---|---|
| Jedi Combo 1 | Mid | Mid | High | High |
| Jedi Combo 2 | Low | Low | Low | Mid |
| Jedi Combo 3 | Mid | Mid | Mid | Low |
| Jedi Combo 4 | Mid | Mid | Mid | High |
| Jedi Combo 5 | High | High | High | Mid |
| Ahsoka Combo 1 | Low | Low | Mid | Low |
| Ahsoka Combo 2 | Mid | Low | Mid | High |
| Ahsoka Combo 3 | Mid | Mid | Low | Low |
| Ahsoka Combo 4 | High | Low | Low | Mid |
| Ahsoka Combo 5 | Low | High | Mid | Mid |

**NOTE**

Once you've stunned a melee enemy, you can execute a combo by performing a variety of high, mid, and low attacks.

## Bio

Ahsoka Tano is Anakin's Padawan, and like her master, she is both highly skilled and overly enthusiastic. She is strong with the Force and is empathetic toward others.

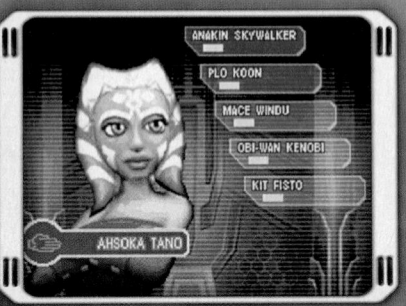

# Anakin Skywalker

## Vitals

**Allegiance:** The Republic

**Rank:** General

**Class:** Jedi Knight

**Species:** Human

**Height:** 1.88

**Force Power:** Combat

## Combo Attacks

| Combo | 1st Hit | 2nd Hit | 3rd Hit | 4th Hit |
| --- | --- | --- | --- | --- |
| Jedi Combo 1 | Mid | Mid | High | High |
| Jedi Combo 2 | Low | Low | Low | Mid |
| Jedi Combo 3 | Mid | Mid | Mid | Low |
| Jedi Combo 4 | Mid | Mid | Mid | High |
| Jedi Combo 5 | High | High | High | Mid |
| Anakin Combo 1 | Mid | Low | High | Low |
| Anakin Combo 2 | Low | Low | Mid | High |
| Anakin Combo 3 | Low | High | Mid | Low |
| Anakin Combo 4 | High | High | Mid | Mid |
| Anakin Combo 5 | High | Mid | Low | Mid |

## Bio

Anakin is a powerful but impetuous Jedi Knight and general. His skills are highly respected by the Jedi Council, but some worry about his unpredictable behavior.

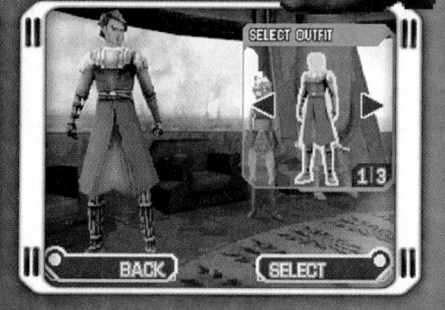

# Kit Fisto

## Vitals

**Allegiance:** The Republic

**Rank:** High General

**Class:** Jedi Knight

**Species:** Nautolan

**Height:** 1.96

**Force Power:** Environmental

## Combo Attacks

| Combo | 1st Hit | 2nd Hit | 3rd Hit | 4th Hit |
|-------|---------|---------|---------|---------|
| Jedi Combo 1 | Mid | Mid | High | High |
| Jedi Combo 2 | Low | Low | Low | Mid |
| Jedi Combo 3 | Mid | Mid | Mid | Low |
| Jedi Combo 4 | Mid | Mid | Mid | High |
| Jedi Combo 5 | High | High | High | Mid |
| Fisto Combo 1 | Low | High | Mid | Mid |
| Fisto Combo 2 | High | Mid | Low | Low |
| Fisto Combo 3 | Low | Mid | High | Mid |
| Fisto Combo 4 | Mid | Low | Mid | Low |
| Fisto Combo 5 | High | High | Mid | High |

## Bio

Kit Fisto is a natural warrior. Equally comfortable fighting on land and in water, he is known for his trademark smile that shows he relishes every moment of battle.

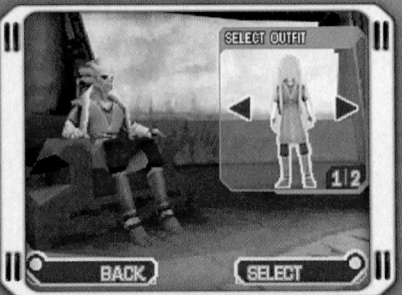

STAR WARS THE CLONE WARS

# Mace Windu

## Vitals

**Allegiance:** The Republic

**Rank:** General

**Class:** Jedi Master

**Species:** Human

**Height:** 1.8

**Force Power:** Combat

## Combo Attacks

| Combo | 1st Hit | 2nd Hit | 3rd Hit | 4th Hit |
|---|---|---|---|---|
| Jedi Combo 1 | Mid | Mid | High | High |
| Jedi Combo 2 | Low | Low | Low | Mid |
| Jedi Combo 3 | Mid | Mid | Mid | Low |
| Jedi Combo 4 | Mid | Mid | Mid | High |
| Jedi Combo 5 | High | High | High | Mid |
| Windu Combo 1 | Low | Mid | Low | Low |
| Windu Combo 2 | Low | Low | High | Mid |
| Windu Combo 3 | High | Mid | Mid | High |
| Windu Combo 4 | Mid | High | High | Low |
| Windu Combo 5 | High | Mid | Low | Mid |

## Bio

Mace Windu is the cool head of the Jedi Council. Mace always seems to have the weight of the galaxy on his shoulders. In truth, he is constantly pondering the depths of the Force.

# Obi-Wan Kenobi

## Vitals

**Allegiance:** The Republic

**Rank:** General

**Class:** Jedi Master

**Species:** Human

**Height:** 1.8

**Force Power:** Combat

## Combo Attacks

| Combo | 1st Hit | 2nd Hit | 3rd Hit | 4th Hit |
|---|---|---|---|---|
| Jedi Combo 1 | Mid | Mid | High | High |
| Jedi Combo 2 | Low | Low | Low | Mid |
| Jedi Combo 3 | Mid | Mid | Mid | Low |
| Jedi Combo 4 | Mid | Mid | Mid | High |
| Jedi Combo 5 | High | High | High | Mid |
| Obi-Wan Combo 1 | Low | Mid | Mid | Low |
| Obi-Wan Combo 2 | Mid | High | High | Mid |
| Obi-Wan Combo 3 | Mid | High | Mid | High |
| Obi-Wan Combo 4 | High | High | Low | Low |
| Obi-Wan Combo 5 | Low | Low | Mid | Mid |

## Bio

Obi-Wan is a seasoned and compassionate warrior and general. His principles and charm make him a natural leader.

# Plo Koon

## Vitals

**Allegiance:** The Republic

**Rank:** General

**Class:** Lifetime member of the Jedi Council

**Species:** Kel Dor

**Height:** 1.88

**Force Power:** Environmental

**NOTE**

At various points in the game, you will also control droids C-3PO and R2-D2. R2-D2 is skilled in zapping droids and tapping security consoles, while C-3PO uses his renowned translation abilities and quick thinking to confuse and irritate the opposition.

## Bio

Plo Koon is a high-ranking general of the grand army of the Republic. He has a strong sense of justice and is highly skilled in hand-to-hand fighting with his lightsaber.

## Combo Attacks

| Combo | 1st Hit | 2nd Hit | 3rd Hit | 4th Hit |
|---|---|---|---|---|
| Jedi Combo 1 | Mid | Mid | High | High |
| Jedi Combo 2 | Low | Low | Low | Mid |
| Jedi Combo 3 | Mid | Mid | Mid | Low |
| Jedi Combo 4 | Mid | Mid | Mid | High |
| Jedi Combo 5 | High | High | High | Mid |
| Koon Combo 1 | Low | Mid | High | Low |
| Koon Combo 2 | Low | Low | Mid | Mid |
| Koon Combo 3 | Mid | Low | Low | Mid |
| Koon Combo 4 | High | High | Mid | Low |
| Koon Combo 5 | Low | Mid | Mid | High |

# THE WAY OF THE SABER

## BASIC CONTROLS

### Movement

Move the stylus on the lower touch screen to move your character in that direction.

### Jumping

Tap on the indicators with your stylus to jump to that location.

### Context-Sensitive Actions

Certain objects will glow to indicate that you can interact with them. Tap on glowing objects with your stylus to perform context-sensitive actions. Some interactive objects can only be found by using the Force ( L or R ).

## COMBAT ACTIONS

### Engaging an Enemy

Upon encountering an enemy, you will automatically draw your lightsaber. At that point, you can engage the foe by tapping on them with your stylus. To disengage from combat, simply tap anywhere on the screen behind you.

### Rapid Attacks

Tap high, mid, or low on an enemy with your stylus to perform rapid attacks with your lightsaber. Some enemies will block these attacks until they are stunned and can only be damaged by performing combo strikes.

### Collecting Items

Walk over an item to automatically collect and use it. Items include health-restoring Ilum crystals and Force orbs, which replenish and add Force power. To collect Force orbs, gather them after breaking destructible containers scattered throughout the levels.

## FORCE ACTION

### Force Push

Hold L or R and tap on an enemy droid with your stylus to perform a Force Push. You can only perform this attack when you are not currently engaged with an enemy and when there is a glow around the intended target.

### Jedi Assist

Tap on the enemy your partner is currently fighting to automatically join in the battle.

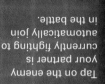

### Deflecting Lasers

Tap on your Jedi as they are about to be hit by a ranged attack to reflect it back to its source.

### Saber Lock

**NOTE**

When fighting melee enemies, you may end up in a Lightsaber Lock with them. Quickly tap anywhere on the screen with your stylus to push the enemy backward to win the lock and prevent your Jedi from taking damage.

**NOTE**

Melee enemies are those that can attack you with melee strikes. Droids, for example, are not melee enemies. Nightsisters are.

### Blocking

Your Jedi will automatically block all attacks as long as they aren't stunned or currently attacking an enemy. However, your Jedi's Defense meter will deplete every time an autoblock is performed.

### Stunning an Enemy

Melee enemies will block your rapid attacks until you breach their defense. In order to breach a melee enemy's defense, you must push them backward by skillfully executing rapid attacks before they have the chance to attack you. Once an enemy is leaning backward, they can be stunned by performing a few more well-timed rapid attacks.

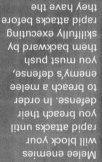

### Reversals

To perform a powerful counter-strike, tap on your Jedi at the moment they are hit by a melee attack.

# Accessing Control Panels

Touch the correct symbol with the stylus and drag it to its matching location when it is the correct color; avoid the other symbols when doing this.

# Team-Up Combat

When your Force meter is full, hold your stylus on an enemy to perform an extremely powerful Team Up Combo. Each time you complete a mission using the same team of Jedi, their bond will strengthen and their Force meter will increase by one segment. The larger your Force meter, the more powerful your Team Up Combos will become, but you must have a full Force meter to use this action, and performing it will use all of your Force power.

# Door Cutting

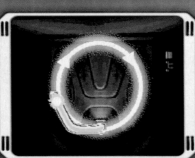

To cut a door open, tap on it with your stylus and draw the pattern that appears.

# Team-Up Environment Ability

At specific points within each mission, there are areas that can only be accessed with the right team of Jedi. Each Jedi is strong in a specific part of the Force, and combining these different strengths will yield varying results.

# R2-D2 Security Tap

With your stylus, tap on the white circle in the screen's center to extend R2-D2's prongs through the openings in each ring.

# MINIGAMES

# Jedi Action Sequences

Use the stylus to trace the patterns that appear onscreen in the direction of the moving cursor.

# A LONG TIME AGO...

## PRELUDE

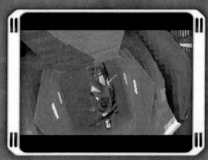

Deep in the far reaches of space, a Jedi cargo ship is under fire. Jedi Master Luminara watches over the cargo as a group of buzz droids cut into the hull and grant an invading ship access to the Jedi transport vessel. As the invading ship boards the Jedi cargo vessel, Master Luminara steps to the front of her clone troops' line with her saber raised and ready for combat. Just then, a mysterious figure disembarks the invading ship. It's a Nightsister...

### TRIVIA BOX

The opening sequence pays homage to the opening shot in *Star Wars: Episode 4—A New Hope*.

## THE SEDAWAN

They came out of nowhere!

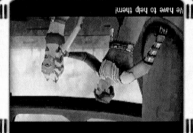

We have to help them!

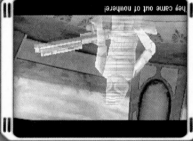

Amidst the turbulence of the Clone Wars years, the Jedi Council receives a distress call from one of its ships, under attack from an unknown enemy. The holo-projection of the clone trooper reports that the ship was overwhelmed, and the stormtroopers could not fend off the invaders. According to Master Kenobi, the ship, the Sedawan, was carrying a load of lightsaber crystals from Ilum. Just as the trooper finishes reporting, the holo-image is interrupted by a flash of a lightsaber cutting across the trooper's gun. Whoever hijacked the Sedawan and stole the crystals is skilled with the saber. Anakin suspects it is Count Dooku, but there is only one way to find out. Investigate.

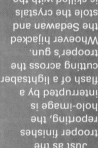

SELECT OUTFIT · 1|3 · BACK · SELECT

Select your two Jedi and proceed.

For the first level, we've selected Anakin Skywalker as our primary Jedi and Ahsoka Tano as his partner.

As you approach the Sedawan on a starfighter, the ship's hull looks surprisingly clean from the outside. Still, you can sense that Master Luminara is in great danger. You land in the Sedawan's hangar bay with your partner in tow.

Walk up to the two crates in the hangar's top left corner and break them open with a few quick 'saber slashes. Near the hangar's bottom right corner are two more crates. Crack them open, then approach the door on the room's north side.

Tap on the blue arrows just in front of the door and you leap onto the raised area. Lead your partner to the door and activate the glowing door switches by tapping on them.

The first few levels have several help holocrons to guide and inform you. Whenever one pops up on the top screen, press (SELECT) to bring up the Help screen.

MOVEMENT
BREAKING OBJECTS
JUMPING
ACTIVATING OBJECTS
ENEMY ENGAGEMENT
CHAIN ATTACKS

BACK ◁ 1/4 ▷

Storm into the corridor ahead and smash through the crates lining the sides of the hall. Go through the door at the hall's far end and enter a shorter, more narrow corridor with red walkways. As soon as you enter, a small group of buzz droids comes rolling out of an adjacent hallway.

Rush the droids and plunge your 'saber into their armor. Leap from droid to droid, assisting your partner as you destroy all droids in the hall. After demolishing the first wave of droids, a second wave will rush out from the hall. Finish them off, and the door at the hall's end will automatically open.

The next area is a large wide-open room with a long winding walkway. On the walkway's opposite side are several more buzz droids. Either deflect their blaster fire back at them from your position, or leap across the walkway to destroy them with several 'saber strikes.

Follow the walkway to the room's northwest corner. Grab the green Ilum crystal there, then use your Force abilities to open the cracked hatch nearby. Proceed through the hatch into the next area.

Once the other platform is lowered, you regain control of the primary Jedi. Backtrack to the walkway along the far left wall and make a right. Follow it to the room's north end and make another right onto the third connecting catwalk. Step on the lowered platform and take it up to the second level, where you reunite with your partner.

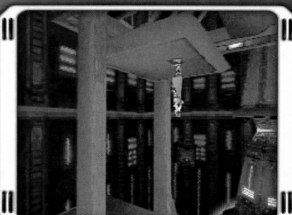

As the second Jedi, rush up the second-level walkway toward the next glowing console. Activate the console to lower the platform on your right to the lower level.

Follow the walkway left, then turn right onto the second catwalk (the first is broken). On the catwalk is a small glowing console. Activate it and your partner will automatically speed by and step onto the a small platform to your right. The platform raises your partner to the second-level walkway, where you then take control of your partner.

The next room is even larger than the previous one. It has several interconnecting walkways with lower and upper levels.

**TIP**

Note that the bottom screen doesn't have a prompt you can "trace," so keep a close eye on the top screen to make sure you're not straying too far from the circle shape.

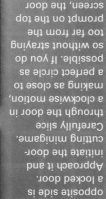

On the room's opposite side is a locked door. Approach it and initiate the door-cutting minigame. Carefully slice through the door in a clockwise motion, making as close to a perfect circle as possible. If you do so without straying too far from the prompt on the top screen, the door will open.

Follow the walkway left, then right to the next hatch. Dash through the doorway into the next room, where several battle droids are going about their business. Take your lightsaber and cut through the rickety droids to clear the room.

In the next hall, cut through crates and cylinders lining the walls and collect the Force orbs they release. Enter the bridge at the hall's end.

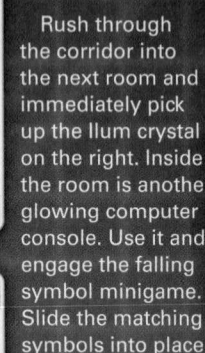

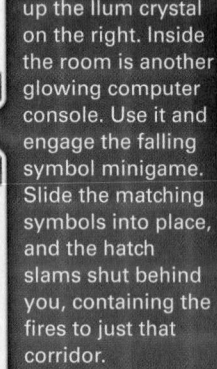

**TRIVIA BOX**

The Sedawan is a tuned-up version of the Rebel blockade runner.

Upon reaching the bridge, you arrive just in time to find that all the escape pods have been jettisoned. Unfortunately, the pods' destinations have been erased from the computer along with the onboard computer memory! Just then, a woman clad in red and toting a red 'saber enters the bridge.

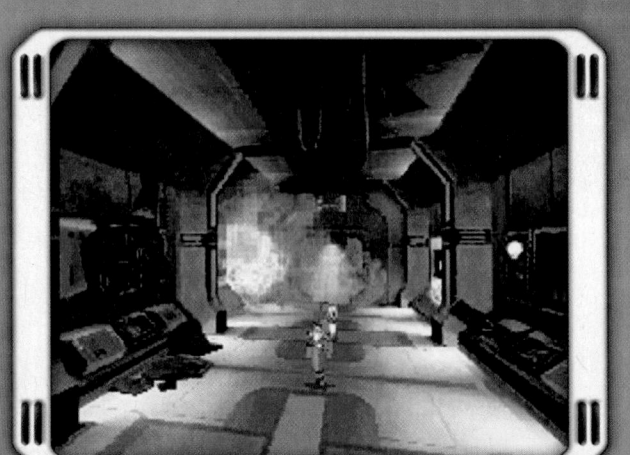

You leap toward her with your lightsaber drawn, but she's too fast. A quick wave of her 'saber sends you and your partner flying backward into the bridge's computers. And just as quickly as she arrived, she disappears back through the hatch through which she entered.

Follow the mysterious woman through the hatch into the next corridor. As you go, the corridor erupts in a series of explosions behind you. The fires threaten to spread to the entire ship unless you find a way to contain them.

Rush through the corridor into the next room and immediately pick up the Ilum crystal on the right. Inside the room is another glowing computer console. Use it and engage the falling symbol minigame. Slide the matching symbols into place, and the hatch slams shut behind you, containing the fires to just that corridor.

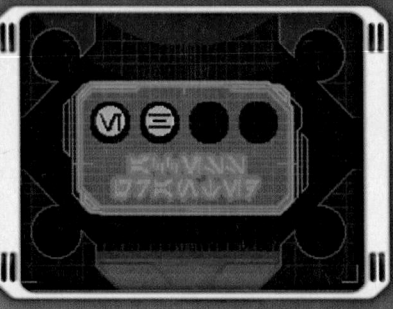

Exit through the doors on the room's left side and you'll enter a Jedi action sequence. The next room is ablaze as the core explodes. Follow the prompts from the Jedi action sequence, and draw an upward diagonal line to leap across the falling debris. While in midair, draw a curved line to slash through the crumbling walkways.

Finally, draw one more curved line to grab the falling walkway and swing to solid ground. You reunite with your partner—who leapt ahead of you—and you speed off, away from the crumbling room.

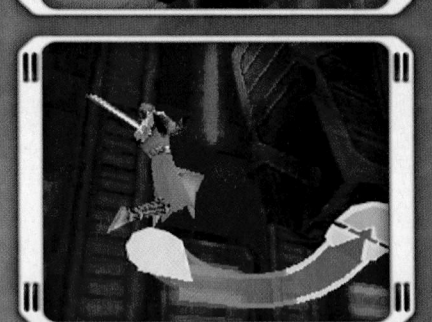

Break open the cylinder in the corridor, then rush into the next room.

Use your Force powers on the blue locking mechanism on the right and open the door in the turret room's bottom left corner. Speed into the corridor and follow it until you find a Sith holocron. Pick it up, then continue to the hall's end. The hall leads to a large cargo bay guarded by several battle droids.

**TIP**

There are two hidden passages in the turret room. To open them, replay the Sedawan level with a different Jedi pair. Use two Jedi with Environmental Force powers to execute a Team Up Environment maneuver and break through the walls.

After destroying the two turrets, walk to the door at the room's bottom left corner.

Step out into the room's center, where the turrets' fires cross. Either deflect their fire back at them or rush the turrets, allowing your saber to block the fire as you go, then cut through the turrets' armor.

Draw one more curved line to leap across the large gap in the room, and land on the far walkway. Dash through the door into the large room with two turrets.

Follow the top walkway left, past the open door, and around the corner into a small room. Pick up the Ilum crystal inside, then backtrack from the room toward the door that opened after you defeated all the droids on the lower level.

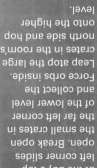

After you clear the bay of all enemies, a door at the bay's top left corner slides open. Break open the small crates in the far left corner of the lower level and collect the Force orbs inside. Leap atop the large crates in the room's north side and hop onto the higher level.

Hold your position near the center of the cargo bay and fend off the second and third waves of buzz droids before they can inflict any damage.

Cut through the small battalion of battle droids and engage the group of buzz droids as they rush in from the right. If you haven't destroyed all the battle droids before the buzz droids arrive, leave the remaining battle droids to your partner while you handle the pesky buzz droids.

Dash into the next room and crush the crates in the corner. Grab the Force orbs they release and pick up the Ilum crystal at the room's far end. Turn left into the long corridor with the orange ribbing. Follow it to the end, breaking the crates as you go. Turn left at the hall's end and enter the hangar.

### CAUTION

If you alert the camera droid by stepping into its light, two battle droids will come storming out of a room nearby. The camera droid will call battle droid duos any time you cross its path, so don't be careless when crossing the room!

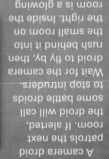

A camera droid patrols the next room. If alerted, the droid will call some battle droids to stop intruders. Wait for the camera droid to fly by, then rush behind it into the small room on the right. Inside the room is a glowing console. Activate the console and successfully complete the falling symbol minigame to bypass the console's security. Activate the console a second time to power up the crane system in the room outside, where the camera droid patrols.

Rush back out into the main room and once again wait for the camera droid to zip by. When it does, head to the room's bottom right corner and activate the glowing console there. This sends the large hanging crate zipping down the room, crashing through the camera droid and busting open the hatch at the end.

Upon entering the hangar, you catch the mysterious lady in red as she boards her ship. She attempts to slow you down by unleashing two of her Nightsisters on you and your partner! Engage the Nightsisters in battle. Use a series of high, mid, and low attacks to assault and deflect the Nightsister's attacks. While you engage one sister, your partner will engage the other, so concentrate on your opponent.

If you engage in a Lightsaber Lock, rapidly tap on your enemy to break the lock, then follow it up with a four-hit combo to inflict major damage. If your partner finishes her opponent before you defeat yours, she'll come to your aid. Use Team Up Combos and your Jedi's special combos to defeat the first pair of Nightsisters.

"I'll take more than the likes of you to stop me."

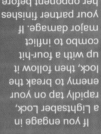

### TRIVIA BOX

The Nightsisters were first referenced in the made-for-TV movie Ewoks: The Battle for Endor.

After defeating the first pair of Nightsisters, a second pair attempts to ambush you. Defeat them as you did the first pair to clean the Sedawan of enemy invaders. Though you defeated the Nightsisters, the mysterious woman in red managed to get away. With your mission complete, there is only one thing left to do. Report to the Jedi Council.

## RODIA

During their investigation on the Sedawan, the Jedi found no trace of its cargo of lightsaber crystals. Instead, they were attacked by a mysterious female who eluded capture. Determined to find their assailant, the Jedi are now heading to the planet Rodia. They report back to the Council that the mysterious woman was strong in the ways of the Force.

Master Yoda is familiar with the woman. She is a Nightsister, and that troubles him deeply. The Jedi report that though the crystals were nowhere to be found, they suspect that they were ejected in the Sedawan's escape pods. The

*...es. And search closer to home we must. A possible ...ly in Coruscant we may have*

investigating Jedi managed to attach a tracking device to the Nightsister's ship as she fled, but the signal was lost after she touched down on Rodia. In the meantime, Yoda also suggests that the Jedi search closer to home as well as inspecting Rodia...

*SELECT OUTFIT*

*1/3*

*BACK    SELECT*

Select a pair of Jedi to proceed.

### NOTE

For the second mission, we've selected Obi-Wan Kenobi and his former Padawan, Anakin Skywalker.

*Don't you worry, Cody. Shield generators are my specialty.*

You speed toward the Rodian city in your transport ship and prepare for landing. Unfortunately, someone has been alerted to your approach and quickly activates the city's dome energy shield. Your A-wing crashes into it just as the dome rises over the city, but your Jedi skills are far too powerful. Just as your ship explodes, you and your partner leap off the ship and free-fall into the city!

Meanwhile, the gunship that was escorting you barely manages to escape the dome. Upon your landing inside the city, your clone comrade Cody contacts you. He can't get through the dome shield. If your troops are going to take the Rodian city, you must first destroy the shield generator.

### TRIVIA BOX

The Devastation battleship is the sister ship to the Malevolence, as featured in the TV shows.

Walk left toward the brown crates and smash them open to grab a few Force orbs. Turn around and walk right, then make a left at the corner. As you walk up the narrow walkway, a group of battle droids storms out of the door ahead and opens fire!

Rush the droids and slash them to bits. After destroying the first wave, backtrack down the walkway to engage the second wave. Help your partner cut them apart, then finish off the final group of droids by the door at the walkway's far end.

Activate the two glowing panels near the door to open it. Before entering the door, your partner expresses some concern over what may lay ahead.

Inside, the large room is separated by a large pool with a submarine floating in the water. Guide your primary Jedi down to the crate in the bottom right corner and crack it open. Take the Force orbs, then dive into the water on your left. Swim across the pool to the room's other side and hop out of the water.

Break open the next crate and cylinder nearby to find an Ilum crystal, then activate the glowing console. This lowers a platform near your partner, and he automatically hops on. The platform rises and carries your partner over a small wall and drops him on the other side, near another glowing console.

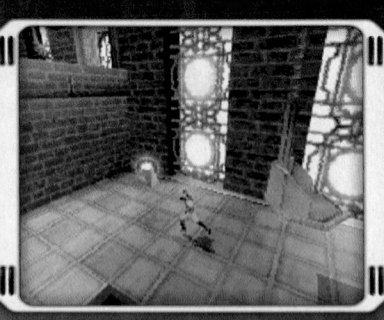

As the second Jedi, activate the glowing console. This time, instead of moving a platform to pick up your partner, the console activates a large magnet that lifts the submarine out of the water. Luckily, the submarine clears a swimming lane deeper into the room where your partner awaits. Hop back into the water and swim under the sub, to the room's north side.

Climb out of the water and approach the glowing console at the room's far north end. Activate it and the room's shutters automatically lock down! The room goes pitch-black, and the large submarine swings around to reveal a blaster turret!

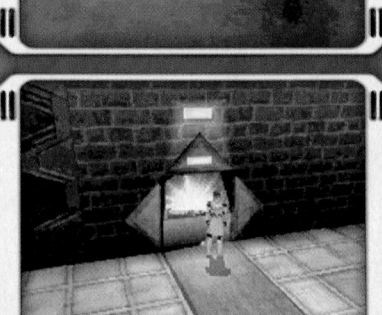

As soon as the turret comes online, your partner ducks behind the pillar on the left. Follow his lead and take cover behind the pillar on the right. Stay behind the pillar as the turret opens fire. When it does, the turret will fire a continuous beam and swing around the room. When the beam swings to your side of the room, your pillar will block it, keeping you safe.

Wait for the turret to cease firing, then rush out from behind your cover and slash at the turret's barrel. When you do, your partner will leap out from his cover and deliver a follow-up blow. Sprint back behind the pillar before the turret opens fire again. Repeat this two more times to defeat the turret.

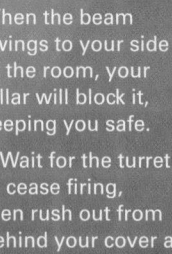
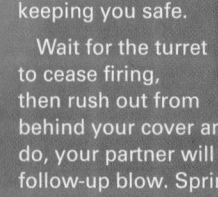
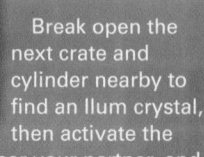

Need a ride?

After destroying the turret, a platform embedded into the north wall drops to ground level.

Step on the platform and activate the glowing control console. This lifts the platform back up to the second level. Break the crates nearby to grab more Force orbs, then follow the walkway right as it leads to an ornate doorway. Go through this door to exit the submarine room.

With the bridge clear, walk over to the control console near the bridge's center and activate it. Match the falling symbols to the three located at the screen's corners, and the dome shield's first generator begins to fail.

Your antics don't go unnoticed. Suddenly, a pair of turrets opens fire on you from the other side of the compound. You duck behind the console, just in time to avoid being hit, but now you're pinned!

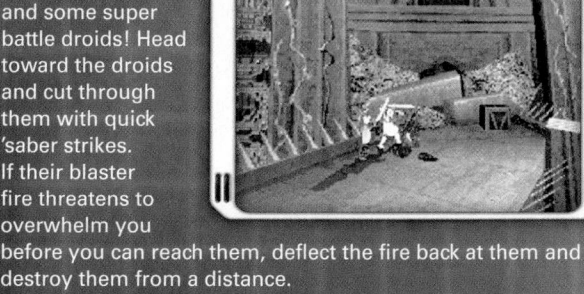

Outside you are greeted by a group of battle droids and some super battle droids! Head toward the droids and cut through them with quick 'saber strikes. If their blaster fire threatens to overwhelm you before you can reach them, deflect the fire back at them and destroy them from a distance.

Follow the Jedi action sequence prompts as they appear on the bottom screen to leap across the canyon and slash the turret cannons off. After destroying the turrets, follow the final prompt to hop down onto a small patch of grass below.

After destroying the first wave, turn around and sprint toward the second wave that appears behind you. Cut through them, melting their metal with your blade, then explore the bridge's far end. Bust open the crates there to find an Ilum crystal.

Dive into the water and swim past the rising and falling mines. Wait until the mine drops, then swim past it and hold your position. When the next mine drops, swim past it and hold again. Continue carefully navigating past the mines until you reach the wall on the other side.

**NOTE**

Don't worry about your partner. They can hit the mines as they swim behind you, but as long as you don't take damage, you'll be able to continue.

At the wall, turn right and swim along the wall's edge. Turn left into the hole in the wall and enter the next area. Here, the robotic mines don't rise and fall; instead they swim left and right. Once again, wait for the mine to pass you by, then quickly swim by it.

Stop before running into the next mine and swim past it as soon as it zips by. Continue doing so until you reach the far end of the underwater cavern. Go through the hole in the cavern's wall and emerge out of the water back in the compound's interior.

After you exit the water, Cody contacts you again. He registers the Rodian shields at 70 percent and has located another generator for you at the top of the tower you're currently in. Destroy the crates nearby to find more Force orbs, and grab the Ilum crystal near the room's opposite side.

After collecting all the loot in the room, walk across the small bridge at the room's center and enter the filtration tower. Again, break all the crates in the room to find more Force orbs.

After collecting all the Force orbs, dive into the pool at the room's center and activate the switch. This makes the tower begin to fill up with water, carrying you to the top!

When the water stops rising, hop out of it and onto the narrow platform along the wall. Follow it left to the exit and walk out of the door to another bridge. Break open the next crate at the bridge, then make a right.

**TIP**

Use the Force while on the catwalk to locate a hidden area. If you have two Jedi with special environmental skills, use their Team Up Environment ability to break through the hidden area and find a Sith holocron.

With the door unlocked, activate the console behind it, and the water begins to rise again.

At the tower's top, get out of the water and climb onto the small catwalk lining the far tower wall. Follow it right, across the tower, to the glowing locked door. Tap the door to drive your lightsaber into it and initiate a door-cutting minigame. Carefully "trace" the prompt on the top screen and draw a circle clockwise on the bottom screen to break the door's lock.

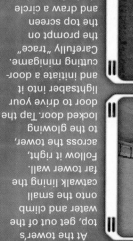

After you destroy the droids, break open all the crates on this side of the bridge. Take the Force orbs, then grab the Ilum crystal near the bridge's far end. Finally, tap on the glowing spot on the shield generator to initiate the symbol-matching minigame. After you complete it successfully, the second generator goes offline.

This time, the droids are guarding the second shield generator. Cut through the droids' ranks and either reflect their blaster fire back at them, or help your partner slash them one by one; whatever you do, dispatch them quickly, or their blaster fire will slowly eat away at your Health bar!

**TRIVIA BOX**

*The game locations Christophsis, Rodia, and Coruscant are all featured in the TV show and in the Clone Wars movie.*

Follow the bridge right until it turns north. Dash toward the small droid battalion ahead. Sever their servos with several saber strikes, then sprint past the pile of parts until you encounter another small group of droids.

Leap from the platform onto the large raised area on the left, then onto the small bridge. Break open the crates here. Collect the Force orbs and Ilum crystal, then approach the console near the bridge's center.

Run along the ledges, leaping from ledge to ledge, as you stay ahead of the turret's blaster fire. Just as you reach the final ledge, the wall behind you begins to crumble and creates a small opening for you to escape. You immediately seize the opportunity and hop down from the ledge into a pool far below.

Swim left to a small platform jutting out into the water and climb out of the water onto solid ground.

Sabotaging the second generator gets you some unwanted heat, and a turret high on the tower opens fire on you! You barely manage to escape by rushing out of the way and onto a series of small broken ledges along the tower's left wall.

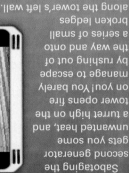

When both floor switches are triggered, the gate on the wall nearby will slide up and reveal a large switch. Tap it and a missing section of the bridge you were previously on rises out of the water and slides into place. Dive back into the water and backtrack onto the bridge. This time, go to the bridge's left end; cross the raised bridge. Make a right at the bridge's far end and drop down onto the narrow walkway leading to the water.

From the safety of the bridge, you spy a large monster swimming in the water below. If you're to continue, you must first trap the monster where he can't hurt you. Wait for the creature to swim under the lower right side of the bridge. When it does, activate the console and close the doors under the bridge, trapping the creature on the other side.

With the monster out of your way, walk to the bridge's right side and hop down to where the monster was previously swimming. Dive into the water and swim to the small platform with the two glowing floor switches on it. Step on one and your partner will automatically step on the other.

Stay calm as it approaches and keep a steady stylus. Follow the onscreen Jedi action sequence prompt when it appears, and dodge the beast's first attack. Follow the second prompt to leap onto the creature's head, and run your saber through its skull!

Follow the walkway right as it leads down to a wide opening. Upon reaching it, you and your partner dive into the water and begin swimming across. Just as you reach the middle of the pool, the large aquatic abomination that you trapped earlier breaks free and attacks!

Dive into the water and swim into the hole left by the megacephalic monster to enter the chamber where you lost the signal from the Night-sister's ship. With no ship in sight, however, you must start looking for clues....

This is where we lost the tracking device signal on the lightsister's ship. She must be around here.

Finally, follow the last prompt to execute an upward slash and cut the beast's belly. The final blow is too much for the monster, and it crashes headfirst into a cracked wall underwater, creating an opening for you to proceed.

**TIP**

If you have a Jedi with a combat specialty and another with an environmental specialty, you can use your Team Up Environment ability to smash through the gate at the bridge's end and to find a Sith holocron.

CORUSCANT

While the search for the unknown female assailant continues on Rodia, the Jedi Council seeks aid on Coruscant. Ziro the Hutt holds the key to this endeavor. However, his palace is uncharacteristically sealed off. Senator Padme Amidala reports to the Jedi Council that her contacts are keeping an eye on Ziro the Hutt. According to them, Ziro always has his ear to the ground when it comes to underground information. Unfortunately, Amidala has been unable to contact Ziro, and his palace is on lockdown.

Master Kit Fisto suspects that the Separatists must be involved. If the Jedi Council is to seek the help of the Nightsister Ros Lai, they must find a way to reach Ziro. With no way of knowing if Ros Lai is even still alive, the Jedi Council has no choice but to infiltrate Ziro's palace. The Jedi Council will send two Jedi to investigate, but Senator Amidala offers to help grant them access by her own means.

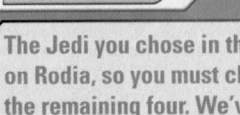
**NOTE**

The Jedi you chose in the second mission are still on Rodia, so you must choose two new Jedi from the remaining four. We've chosen Jedi Masters Plo Koon and Mace Windu, respectively.

While you're selecting your Jedi duo, Senator Amidala sends her two droids, C-3PO and R2-D2, into Ziro the Hutt's palace. The two droids calmly walk up to the palace doors and knock. A Separatist Magna guard opens the door and captures Padme's protocol pals. Just then, you arrive with your partner at Ziro's palace with no way to get in.

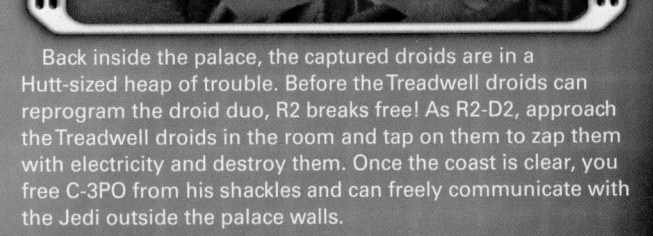

Back inside the palace, the captured droids are in a Hutt-sized heap of trouble. Before the Treadwell droids can reprogram the droid duo, R2 breaks free! As R2-D2, approach the Treadwell droids in the room and tap on them to zap them with electricity and destroy them. Once the coast is clear, you free C-3PO from his shackles and can freely communicate with the Jedi outside the palace walls.

Zap the four crates scattered about the room to break them and collect the Force orbs inside. Then approach the glowing lock near the room's far left corner, and hack it to activate the R2 minigame. In this minigame, wait until the spinning gaps in the spinning rings are lined up with the center lock-picking mechanism. When it does, tap on the center lock-picking mechanism to deploy the rods through the openings in the outer rings. Do this to all three rings before the time runs out and the door will unlock, granting the Jedi access into Ziro's palace! (You automatically switch back to the Jedi at this point.)

The little droid's efforts pay off, and you gain access to the palace. Once inside Ziro's bar, you find that the palace is almost entirely empty. One of Ziro's Bith servants spots you and runs off. You immediately alert C-3PO that you've been spotted so that he can stop the sniveling Bith if he attempts to alert someone.

Certainly, sir. But I'm not entirely sure how we might do that. After all, I am merely a protocol droid.

Break the cylinders nearby and grab the Force orbs and the Ilum crystal in Ziro's bar, then stand on the small glowing circle on the ground. When you do, your primary Jedi stands on the circle while you take control of the secondary Jedi. Use the Force to move the small pedestal on the

right, then step on the glowing circle revealed by the pedestal. The force field around the pedestal on the left deactivates.

Back in control of your primary Jedi, press the button on the left pedestal. The wall at the bar's rear opens to reveal a hidden passage. Rush into the corridor and bust open the cylinders and crates at the end of the first hall. Make a right at the hall's end, breaking crates as you go, and pass under the small archway into a new hallway.

As soon as you enter, the hallway ahead is sealed off by several red laser gates. You're trapped! You attempt to contact R2 only to find that the trap is interfering with your communications signal. (You now shift to controlling C-3PO.)

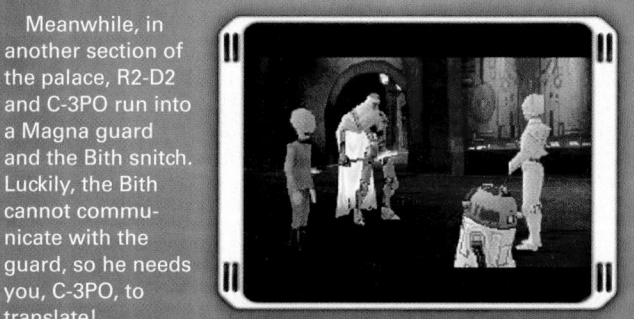

trap!

**TRIVIA BOX**

**The Sedawan and the Devastation were designed exclusively for the game.**

Meanwhile, in another section of the palace, R2-D2 and C-3PO run into a Magna guard and the Bith snitch. Luckily, the Bith cannot communicate with the guard, so he needs you, C-3PO, to translate!

Respond with the following commands to trick the guard and betray the Bith:

He says there are Jedi in the palace.

He says that there are intruders in the palace.

He says that the jazz band is late.

1. "He says that the jazz band is late."

2. "They owe him credits and he demands that you assist him in their collection!" or "He says that no matter is too trivial when it comes to credit collection!"

Walk to the end of the next hall, past the two control consoles on the right, and break open the cylinders there. Backtrack to the two consoles and destroy them to drop the laser gate, then proceed into the next corridor.

Just as you enter the hangar, you spy several Magna guards on the level above. Without hesitation, they leap down for the attack!

As the Jedi, turn left in the hall and walk to its end. Break open the crates at the hall's end, then backtrack to the main passage. Carefully approach the malfunctioning gate and wait for the lasers to turn off. When they do, rush through the opening before they reactivate. Make a right in the next hall, and destroy the two consoles flanking the next laser gate to deactivate it.

Break open the two cylinders at the hall's end to find more Force orbs, then backtrack to the hall's center and take the passage on the left. The hall ends at a T-intersection. On the right are two more crates; break them open for more Force orbs, then make a left past the next malfunctioning laser gate.

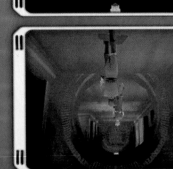

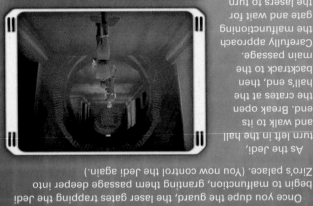

Once you dupe the guard, the laser gates trapping the Jedi begin to malfunction, granting them passage deeper into Ziro's palace. (You now control the Jedi again.)

3. "As a simple guard, he demands you assist him immediately or he will report you!" or "He inquires if you need a memory wipe, as your behavior pattern must be faulty."
4. "He wonders if you would be more suited to work as a speed bump."
5. "He swears you are the sorriest excuse for a droid and would be more useful melted down."

Make a left at the hall's end and dash past the next broken laser gate. Bust open the cylinders just behind the broken laser gate and collect a few more Force orbs. Next, speed past two more malfunctioning laser gates on the left.

**TIP**

Another Sith holocron is visible just behind the metal grating at the hall's end. To grab it, use a Team Up Environment ability with two combat specialty Jedi.

Break two more cylinders on the corridor's south side, then break the console on the corridor's north end to bring down the next laser gate. Finally, break the final two cylinders in the corridor ahead before making a left, grabbing the Ilum crystal on the ground, and exiting into the main hangar.

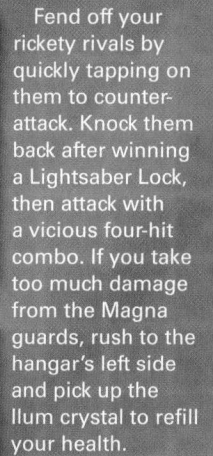

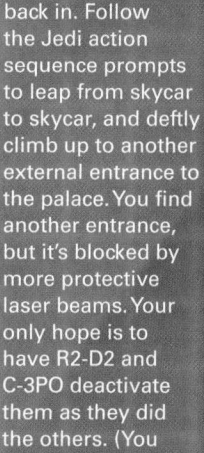

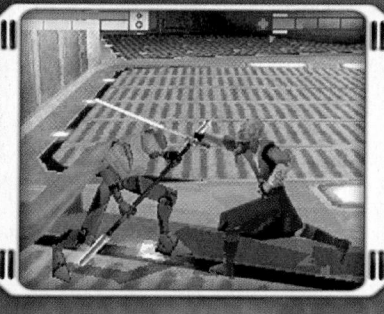

Fend off your rickety rivals by quickly tapping on them to counter-attack. Knock them back after winning a Lightsaber Lock, then attack with a vicious four-hit combo. If you take too much damage from the Magna guards, rush to the hangar's left side and pick up the Ilum crystal to refill your health.

Once you're replenished, rejoin the fight and help your partner finish off the first wave of Separatist robots. After destroying the first wave, a second and third wave of guards arrives, itching for a fight. Give it to them, and finish them off quickly with Jedi assist attacks and team-up combos.

**TIP**

After destroying the Magna guards, grab the Sith holocron on the hangar's upper level. To reach it, use a Team Up Environment ability with two environmental Jedi on the ship in the hangar. Once you move it into place, you can jump on it, and then to the upper level.

With the hangar free from enemy resistance, head over to the control panels on the hangar's far right corner and activate them to drop the laser gate on the right. The large landing pad leads back out to the busy skyways surrounding Ziro's palace.

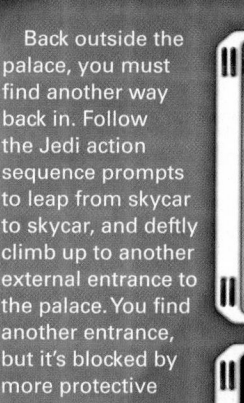

Back outside the palace, you must find another way back in. Follow the Jedi action sequence prompts to leap from skycar to skycar, and deftly climb up to another external entrance to the palace. You find another entrance, but it's blocked by more protective laser beams. Your only hope is to have R2-D2 and C-3PO deactivate them as they did the others. (You now take control of R2-D2.)

Back in the palace, R2-D2 and C-3PO are under attack from more Treadwell droids. Tap on them to zap them with electricity and dispatch them.

As R2-D2, roll into the hall on the far left corner. As you go, a trio of Treadwells will try to stop you. Fry their circuits as they approach and continue up the hall until you enter the next control room. Inside are another trio of Treadwells. Fry them like you did their companions, then grab the Ilum crystal in the room's far end.

Glide over to the control panel on the room's left and initiate another R2-D2 minigame. Slide the bolt through the spinning rings and unlock the doors blocking your Jedi buddies.

The planet Dathomir is the home of the Nightsisters. The planet was uniquely redesigned to match the style of the TV Show.

With R2-D2 holding up his end of the plan, you can sneak back into the palace—only to find another blocked passageway! Luckily, this is one you can handle. Walk up to the purple window on the right and use the Force to flip the switch on the other side. This deactivates the laser gates on your side of the passage but activates the laser gates on the other side.

Once the gates are dropped, step into the room on the left and break open the crates inside. Take the Force orbs, then activate the control consoles in the room to bring up the window shutters. When the window shutters rise, they expose the switch on the window's other side. Once again, flip the switch to deactivate the laser gates behind you.

Walk into the next tunnel where a pair of large fans are spinning.

NOTE

If you have a combat and an environmental Jedi pair, you can execute a Team Up Environment ability to break open the door on the left and grab a Sith holocron.

With no way to get past the spinning fans in one piece, you contact R2-D2 and ask him to hack the fan controls. Back in the control room, as C-3PO, sneak past the camera droid, using the niches along the wall to hide in, and activate the glowing switch at the hall's far right end.

The switch unlocks the cell door. Backtrack to the control room (head south), where you'll take control of R2-D2. Activate the glowing console in the room's far right corner and slow the fans to a manageable speed. Well, manageable for Jedi, anyway...

NOTE

If the camera droid spots you as sneak by, you'll have to restart the sneaking sequence!

Ventress wastes little time in attacking. Before you can act, she assaults you with a Sith lightning attack! Dodge her attack by running away, and instead destroy one of her battle droid companions. Once the droid is downed, use the Force to hurl the droid's broken body at her. The blow knocks her off guard and creates an opening for you to attack.

Rush Ventress while she's stunned. Use combination 'saber strikes and mulithit combos to whittle her health away. As you attack, keep a close watch on your Team-up Combo meter. When it's full, unleash a team-up combo to dish out major

Back in the fan tunnel, carefully approach the first fan and use the Force to target it. Tap on the fan to destroy the blades with a Force attack, then rush past it. Do the same to the second fan, and grab the Ilum crystal on the ground. Turn right at the tunnel's end and jump down into the shaft leading to Ziro's throne room.

When you arrive, you find Ziro the Hutt shackled! He begs you to "make her stop," but who is "she"? Just then, you get your answer. Asajj Ventress, Dooku's dome-headed drone.

damage. Repeat this process several times until Ventress retreats like the coward she is.

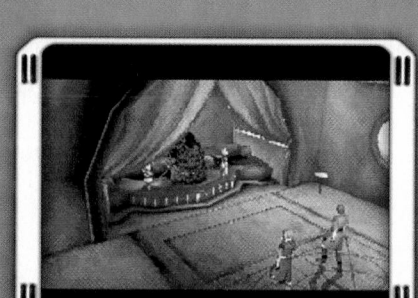

With Ventress gone, Ziro the Hutt is very grateful. Before he can offer you his deepest thanks, however, a mysterious woman in blue drops in from the vents. It's Ros Lai!

After much deliberation, and with some hesitation, Ros Lai agrees to help you, as long as you can smuggle her off Coruscant. Reluctant though she may be, you've made your first ally in the fight against Dooku and the Nightsisters....

# RETURN TO RODIA

Rush the Night-sisters and lash out at them with your lightsaber. Destroy the first three Nightsisters with your partner's help, then fend off the next two waves of attackers. Use several multihit combos and team-up combos to dispatch them quickly, then walk up to the hatch on the north wall.

As the Council begins their analysis of the intercepted Night-sister transmission on Ros Lai's data chip, the Jedi find themselves digging deeper into the planet Rodia in their hunt for the female attacker from the Sedawan. Back on the planet Rodia, the two Jedi sent to investigate contact the clone commander Cody. Instead of getting a reply, though, they get nothing but static. The shield is interfering with communications between the Jedi generals and their troops.

Before the Jedi can figure out a way to contact their clone troops, the pool from which they emerged into the Rodian compound is sealed off. The Jedi draw their 'sabers as the mysterious Nightsister drops in from above with a small group of Nightsister lackeys! Before they can stop her, the Night-sister leader escapes through a tunnel at the chamber's north end, leaving her followers to fend off the Jedi.

Activate the two consoles near the wall to open the hatch.

**NOTE**

You pick up the adventure with the same pair of Jedi you chose at the beginning of your second mission.

Enter the long blue tunnel and sprint north. Follow the tunnel until you're ambushed by a small group of Nightsisters. Hold your position and fight off the nasty Nightsisters. Act quickly—you're outnumbered!

Make a right into the hall at the tunnel's end. Follow the hall to its end and enter the large storehouse. Break all the crates and cylinders there to find plenty of Force orbs. Press the glowing button on the console near the room's far end and successfully complete the symbol-matching minigame.

While you deactivate the final shield generator, the lead Nightsister unleashes more of her minions on you. The group of Nightsister lackeys waits for you in the large tunnel you used to enter the storehouse. Don't disappoint them; backtrack to the tunnel and meet them in combat.

**TIP**

After entering the small hall before the storehouse, turn left down the adjacent hall. If you have two environmental/combat Jedi, use your Team Up Environment ability to open the doors at the hall's end. Grab the Sith holocron, then backtrack to the main hall.

After defeating the group of Nightsisters in the tunnel, walk to the hatch near the tunnel's middle and activate the door-cutting minigame. This time, instead of a circle, draw an upside-down triangle and cut the door open.

Rush inside and stop at the hall's corner. Farther down the hall to the right, a turret opens fire on you! Rush into the hall, allowing your lightsaber to deflect the incoming fire, and either duck into the hall on the left or reflect the turret's fire back at it.

**CAUTION**

Though you can reflect the turret's fire back at it to destroy it, the turret's extremely tough. Only the most experienced Jedi should attempt to destroy the turret in this fashion.

Break the crates open in the large room, then use the console against the far wall. Complete the symbol-matching minigame to disable the turret in the hall (if you haven't already destroyed it).

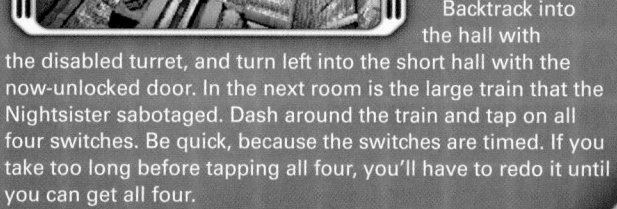

Backtrack out to the hall with the now-disabled turret and make a left. Walk north to the hall's end. As you enter the room there, the Nightsister leader sabotages the train generator. She sprints away before you can catch her, but you formulate a plan to catch up to the speedy sister. Activate the two consoles in the room to unlock the door in the hall behind you.

Backtrack into the hall with the disabled turret, and turn left into the short hall with the now-unlocked door. In the next room is the large train that the Nightsister sabotaged. Dash around the train and tap on all four switches. Be quick, because the switches are timed. If you take too long before tapping all four, you'll have to redo it until you can get all four.

After flipping all four switches, the train takes off like a laser bolt and you speed after the fleeing Nightsister.

The dastardly Nightsister realizes you've given chase and immediately booby-traps the train tracks with droids! Follow the prompts for the Jedi action sequence to cut through the droids, leap off the train, and narrowly avoid a head-on collision with a second train. Upon landing safely at the train station, you're reunited with your partner, who also narrowly missed the collision.

At least they're not trying to kill us like everything

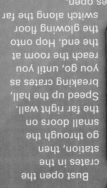

Bust open the crates in the station, then go through the small doors on the far right wall. Speed up the hall, breaking crates as you go, until you reach the room at the end. Hop onto the glowing floor switch along the far wall, and the small hatch on the floor slides open.

While your primary Jedi stands on the floor switch, you take control of the secondary Jedi. Jump into the pool revealed by the open floor panels. Just as you dive into the water, a group of Night-sisters ambushes your partner on the floor switch!

Rendezvous with your partner and flip the other switch on the wall to open the hatch at the tunnel's end.

There's nothing you can do about it now. The floor panels slide shut and you're underwater. Follow the underwater tunnel as it wends around. Stop at the laser gates and wait for them to disable before proceeding past them. At the tunnel's end, swim to the wall switch and activate it. When you do, the floor panels open again, and you revert back to controlling the primary Jedi. Cut the Night-sister attackers to ribbons with quick combos and fierce 'saber slashes. After you defeat them all, hop down onto the main floor and dive into the pool after your partner.

Lead your partner deeper into the tunnel, past more malfunctioning laser gates. When you reach the tunnel's end, you rise out of the water into another large chamber. Once again, a small swarm of Nightsisters ambushes you.

Defend against their attack and counter with combos. Defeat the Nightsisters, then activate the two glowing consoles at the chamber's far end.

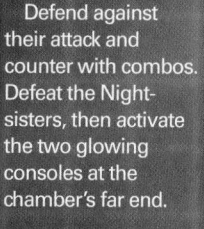

Follow the corridors, breaking boxes as you go, and collect the Force orbs and Ilum crystal in the first room. Make a right into the hall and follow it until you reach the control room.

Though the Nightsister manages to stay one step ahead of you, you're getting closer. Leave the control room through the door on the right and you'll automatically leap down to the area below and engage the first group of battle droids. Slash them to little bits, then dash left across the bridge.

On the bridge's other side, flip the two glowing switches and go through the door into the next hallway. Sprint to the room at the hall's end and break open all the crates inside.

Flip the switch on the console at the room's end and successfully complete the falling-symbol minigame. This unlocks the door on the left side of the control room.

Backtrack out of the room, down the hall, and back to the bridge. There, you encounter several more Nightsisters. Swashbuckle past them on the bridge and destroy the Nightsisters before they can defeat you.

Dash back into the control room, then go through the door on the left.

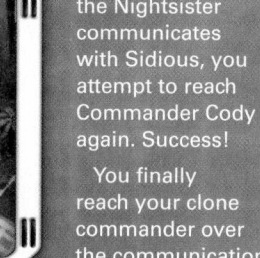

Speed into the corridor on the left and follow it to its end. There, you finally catch up to the Nightsister and spy her communicating with Darth Sidious! She reports that the stolen crystals are absorbing the Force energy as expected. While the Nightsister communicates with Sidious, you attempt to reach Commander Cody again. Success!

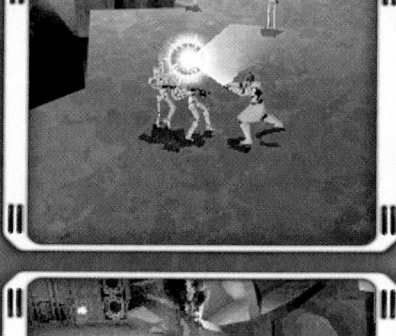

My fellow Nightsisters have taken care of them.

You finally reach your clone commander over the communications channel. Cody breaks through the shield and zeroes in on your position, but the gunship rocks the compound and exposes your position to the Nightsister!

Commander Cody, come in.

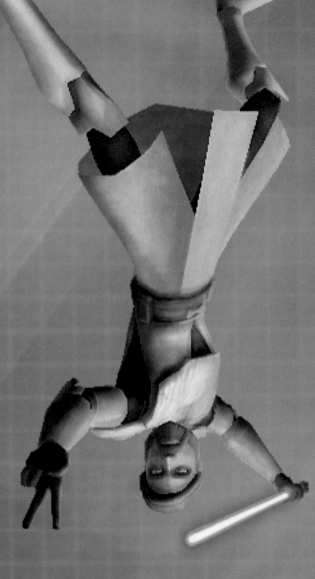

Without a moment's hesitation, the Nightsister attacks.

**TRIVIA BOX**

The voices in the game are from the same actors as the TV show.

The Nightsister attacks from high above the ground. You can't reach her, so instead of wagging your lightsaber at her feet, attack the large crystal at the center of the large chamber. With each blow of your saber, the crystal shoots smaller needlelike shards around the room. After knocking three crystal shards to the floor, use the Force to hurl them at the high-flying fiend.

After you hit the Nightsister three times, she falls to the floor, helpless. Rush the Nightsister and attack with a flurry of combos. When she's taken enough, the Nightsister floats back up and resumes attacking you with lightning blasts. Dodge her attacks and repeat the crystal and combos attacks until you defeat her.

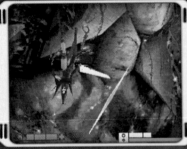

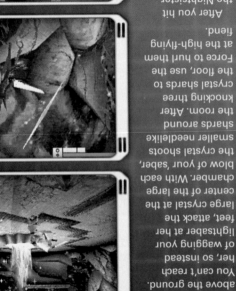
Our arrogance will be your downfall!

So nice of you to drop in, Jeedai. A pity you won't be

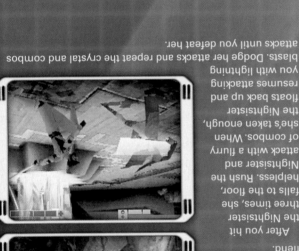

# CHRISTOPHSIS

Deeply troubled by the discovery that the Night-sisters are in league with Dooku, the Jedi Council has once again enlisted Senator Amidala's help. The analysis of Ros Lai's information points toward the planet Christophsis, where the senator's covert probes have confirmed the Council's suspicions. As Amidala reports on her findings—that the Separatists are mining for something on Christophsis—her transport ship crashes!

The Jedi Council watches as the senator's holo-image is disrupted and goes offline. In a panic, Anakin demands that the Council send help. The Council agrees...

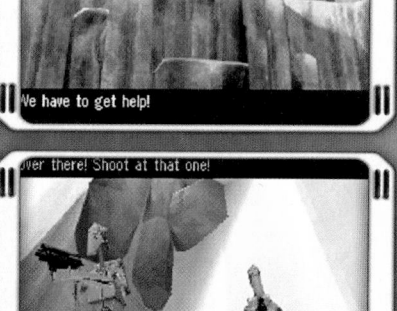

As your dropship approaches the landing point on Christophsis, you encounter resistance. What at first seems like a beacon is actually incoming fire, and the ship is shot down. It crashes on the edge of a precipice and hangs precariously. Before you can act, a small group of battle droids arrives and opens fire on the ship.

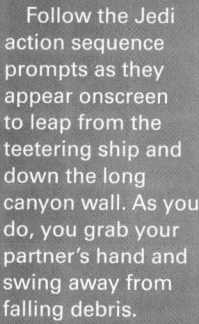

Follow the Jedi action sequence prompts as they appear onscreen to leap from the teetering ship and down the long canyon wall. As you do, you grab your partner's hand and swing away from falling debris.

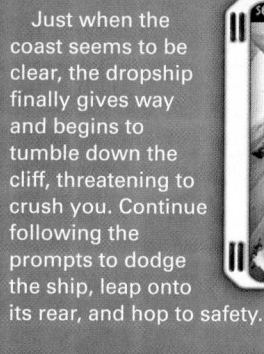

Just when the coast seems to be clear, the dropship finally gives way and begins to tumble down the cliff, threatening to crush you. Continue following the prompts to dodge the ship, leap onto its rear, and hop to safety.

Select a pair of Jedi before proceeding.

We've selected Obi-Wan Kenobi and Anakin Skywalker.

You land safely on a ledge leading into the heart of the cliffside, but your thoughts are on your ship's crew and leader, Commander Kree. The commander doesn't respond to your message, so you've no choice but to continue on your mission.

Commander Gree, come in!

Clear the room, then grab the Ilum crystal on the ground. Break the remaining crates and cylinders, then go through the door on the north wall. This leads to an elevator that quickly begins to rise, carrying you high into the cavern before coming to a screeching halt. You've been detected! As the battle droids prepare to open fire, successfully complete the cutting minigame and carve out a hole in the base of the elevator floor.

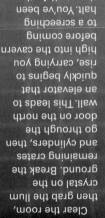

Complete the Jedi action sequence to safely leap down the elevator shaft and land on the ground floor of the massive compound.

The ground floor leads to an exit. Walk outside and break open all the crates nearby. Double-jump onto the walkway on the left, then storm onto the narrow bridge, battling Nightsisters and droids as you go.

First destroy the bothersome Nightsisters, then focus on the droids. While you dispatch the Nightsisters, the droids can safely land on the bridge and become easier to hit.

Crush the crate on the ledge, then step into the dark passageway ahead. Break open all the crates in the cave and approach the blast doors at the cave's end. Run your saber into the door and trace an upside-down triangle to cut through the lock. Run into the next section of the cave, still breaking open the crates as you go, until you reach a room full of droids.

Blast doors in a cave?

Crush the first few droids, then speed to the small glowing pillar on the left. Target it with the Force and destroy the pillar to bring the wall above it crumbling down. As it does, it blocks the transport hole for more droids! Destroy the pillar on the left as well, then finish off the remaining droids in the cavern.

**TIP**

On the cavern's east side, before you enter the elevator, two pillars block a hidden area. Use a Team Up Environment ability with two combat Jedi to gain access to a Sith holocron.

If a droid is out of reach, use the Force to bring it down. With the bridge free of all enemies, cross it to the right, break open the containers, and collect the Force orbs. Turn left at the bridge's far end and follow it north to the large glowing panel at the end. Successfully complete the symbol-matching minigame, and three large pillars appear below, bridging the gap on the bottom floor.

### TRIVIA BOX

**The games cart size is a massive 256 megabytes!**

Backtrack across the bridge and defeat the second wave of Night-sisters.

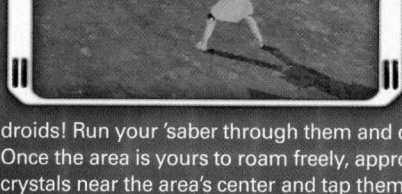

Hop back down to the ground floor and make a left. Hop across the newly risen pillars and reach the other side of the large chasm. There, activate the two glowing panels and head back inside the caves. Trek deeper into the caves, breaking the containers as you go. Collect the Force orbs, then exit back out to a large wide-open area.

There, you are ambushed by more Nightsisters and droids! Run your 'saber through them and dispatch them quickly. Once the area is yours to roam freely, approach the three large crystals near the area's center and tap them one by one.

### TIP

Grab the Ilum crystal on the area's left side before proceeding.

Tapping the three crystals activates them and sends three bright blue lights into the nearby cliffside. The cliff crumbles, creating a pillared path up the cliffside.

Hop up the pillars until you reach the entrance to the next cave. Enter and break the containers as you go. When you reach a bridge, you're ambushed again! This time, the Nightsisters bring a new friend to the battle. The blue Nightsister is a ranged-attack specialist. Dispatch her first, then take out the other pesky sisters.

Continue crossing the bridge until you're greeted by a friendly dropship. It's Commaner Kree; he and the crew of your dropship survived! You command him to find a landing area while you continue the search for Senator Amidala.

We're still searching for Padmé. Find a landing site nearby and we'll contact you once we have her

More of these crystals.

Finish crossing the bridge and open the door at the end by flipping both switches. The next room is a large glowing chamber with two doors, one on each side, and three huge glowing crystals.

Walk up to the base of the left crystal and wait for the room to glow green. When it does, press the button on the crystal's base to unlock the green door. Rush out onto the long catwalk and engage the twisted sisters! Fight past the swarm of Night-sisters until you reach the walkway's other side.

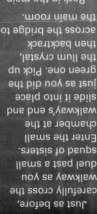

Enter the room there, then use the Force to slide the small crystal pillar back. Once this crystal in place, the center crystal in the large glowing chamber is surrounded by a rising pedestal.

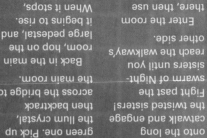

> **NOTE**
>
> You must defeat all the Nightsisters on the catwalk so that the door to the small pillar chamber will open.

Grab the Ilum crystal behind the small pillar, then backtrack across the walkway to the glowing chamber.

This time, open the blue door by tapping the right crystal when the room glows blue.

---

Just as before, carefully cross the walkway as you duel past a small squad of sisters. Enter the small chamber at the walkway's end and slide it into place just as you did the green one. Pick up the Ilum crystal, then backtrack across the bridge to the main room.

Back in the main room, hop on the large pedestal, and it begins to rise. When it stops, creep into the corridor, break the crates in your way, and turn right at the end.

> **TIP**
>
> At the corridor's end, near where you turn right, there is a translucent wall. Use a Team Up Environment ability with two environmental Jedi to remove the panel and pick up the Sith holocron.

es, but the Captain requires medical attention.

We overheard the guards saying something about the separatists harvesting crystals from the planet core.

Use the glowing consoles to enter the final room and find the senator, her clone comrade, C-3PO, and R2-D2 all behind laser gates. You deactivate the laser gate and free them from their prison, but there's no time to rejoice.

The senator overheard her captors talk about harvesting crystals from the planet core. The Separatists' plans are even more sinister than first thought. First they stole the lightsaber crystal cargo, and now they're harvesting them from the planet? With no time to waste, you contact Commander Kree and call for an evac. Your mission here is complete...for now.

> **TRIVIA BOX**
>
> Adegan crystals are from the planet Ilum and are the power source of a lightsaber.

# DATHOMIR

Select a pair of Jedi from the four remaining. The Jedi pair sent to Chris-tophsis remains there, so you can't choose them again. We've chosen Plo Koon and Ahsoka Tano.

TRIVIA BOX

**Ilum was featured in the original *Clone Wars* cartoons.**

The alliance between Dooku and the Night-sisters troubles the Council deeply. The only place left to go is to the source itself—Dathomir, home of the Night-sisters.

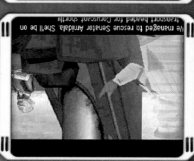

n the meantime, we'll continue to investigate.

Hmm. Most troubling is this alliance between the Nightsisters, and Dooku's Separatists. Analyze Ros Lai's

We managed to rescue Senator Amidala. She'll be on transport headed for Coruscant shortly

The successful rescue of Senator Amidala on Chris-tophsis brings confirmation of the Separatists' interest in the crystals on the planet. However, much to the Jedi Council's dismay, Ros Lai's information is incomplete. It is in this moment of uncertainty that Yoda reveals what the Jedi's next move should be. While Senator Amidala is en route to Coruscant, the Jedi report to the Council.

Approach the compound's side door and step on the long yellow floor switch. When you do, your partner steps on the second switch and the doors slide open. You step into a large chamber with a small pool of water separating the room and a retracted bridge at the center. Step on the floor switch at the room's bottom right corner. This opens an underwater hatch and passes control to your secondary Jedi.

Upon landing on Dathomir, your clone scout spies several squads of battle droids accompanied by Nightsisters. In order to bypass the security, the scout suggests you infiltrate the facility through a side entrance. You agree and storm into the compound's side entrance while the clones hold position and create a diversion.

here's a lot of activity down there, sir. I count at least 4 squads of battle droids and some of those

As the secondary Jedi, dive into the water and swim through the newly opened hatch.

Upon reaching the other side of the underwater tunnel, your primary Jedi is attacked by Nightsisters! He steps off the floor switch, and the water on your side of the tunnel rises. Get out of the water and rush through the door on the right to aid your partner.

Back in the entry chamber, you can see your partner surrounded by Nightsisters. Dash to the control console at the chamber's bottom left and activate it. Complete the symbol-matching game to extend the bridge at the room's center, which connects both sides of the chamber.

In the second chamber, where your secondary Jedi emerged from the water, step on the two floor switches to open the door on the left. Pick up the Ilum crystal in the hall and head down the passage until you're reunited with your clone troopers. A trooper reports that they were ambushed and overwhelmed. Despite the trooper's seemingly broken spirit, you command him to soldier up and get into a tight

formation so that the troops can cover your advance into the compound.

Rush into the next chamber and engage the Nightsisters in battle. They're holding more of your clone troopers hostage! As you fight the Nightsisters, grab the two Ilum crystals in the chamber to replenish your health. Quickly destroy the several waves of Nightsisters and reunite your trooper squadron. Once you do, break all the orange tablets in the chamber to find some Force orbs.

Once you're rejoined with your partner, you resume control over the primary Jedi. Quickly fend off the attacking Nightsisters and cross left over the bridge.

**CAUTION**

The black-clad Nightsisters are highly skilled with the lightsaber. They'll counterattack after your combos, so be careful!

Walk up to the door on the chamber's far right and rendezvous with your clone troopers. The troopers report that they've detected a high amount of activity underground. The door on the far right will lead you toward it. However, in order to proceed, you need to distract the forces inside the compound. Your troopers agree to provide cover fire.

While crossing the first bridge, you encounter several more breakable objects containing Force orbs along the far left wall. Leap from the bridge to the left wall to grab them, then leap back to the bridge to continue on your mission.

As the secondary Jedi, leap into the pool and carefully swim past the blinking laser gates. Wait for the lasers to deactivate, then quickly swim past them. Once on the other side, get out of the water and step onto one of the floor switches. Once in place, take control of the primary Jedi and swim past the laser gates to join your partner on the second floor switch. The floor switches open a door on the room's opposite side.

Go through the door and up the corridor. Stop to destroy the tablets near the end, then enter the next chamber. Before leaving the large chamber, explore the room's west side. If you have one environmental Jedi and one combat Jedi, use a Team Up Environment ability on the wall to reveal a Sith holocron.

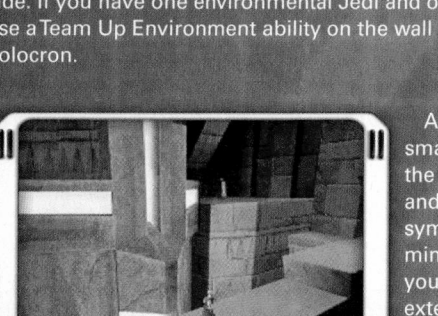

Activate the small console near the retracted bridge and complete the symbol-matching minigame. When you do, the bridge extends across the wide gap and connects the two sides of the chamber. Dash across the bridge into the next large chamber.

Swim back across the small pool and break the tablets on the room's other side, then go through the newly opened door. There is an Ilum crystal just right after entering the room, but don't get it just yet. Instead, wait for the Nightsisters to drop in from above. When they do, rush at them and unleash your 'saber combos.

Use Team Up Combos to dispatch them quickly. Grab the Ilum crystal midfight if you take too much damage. After surviving the Nightsister ambush, walk up to the door on the far left and stand on the floor switches nearby to open it.

As you cross the small walkway in the next chamber, an explosion from below crumbles the walkway underneath your feet. Follow the

Jedi action sequence prompts to safely navigate the falling rubble, and dodge the booby traps along the walls. Upon landing on the bottom of the tall chamber, you spy a pool guarded by laser gates.

Before leaving the room where you were ambushed, move north to the edge of the gap between the main floor and the center spire. Use a Team Up Environment ability with two combat Jedi to topple the center stone spire. Then jump to the other side of the fallen spire to find a Sith holocron.

Rush down the next hallway, collecting the Illum crystal as you go. When you reach the next room—a large coffin-filled chamber—a pair of Nightsisters saunters in from the opposite end. Without warning, they leap into action! Destroy the Nightsister attackers, then break the tablets in the room's corners. After collecting the Force orbs, hop down onto the main floor of the coffin-filled chamber.

As soon as you set foot on the lower level, more Nightsisters drop in from above. As you whittle their numbers down, also break the tablets and small spires on the bottom floor to collect more Force orbs.

Flip the two glowing switches near the room's north wall to open the door on the chamber's upper level.

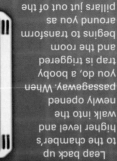

Follow the winding tunnel as it leads deeper into the compound. As you go, break the small spires lining the walls to find more Force orbs. After making the first turn, follow the tunnel to its end, where a fallen piece of debris blocks a hidden door. Use a Team Up Environment ability with two environmental Jedis to reveal a secret chamber with a Sith holocron.

Follow the onscreen prompts to successfully complete the Jedi action sequence, and bound up and out of the booby-trapped room. Once you're safely across the booby trapped room, break the two tablets flanking the doorway and enter the passage on the far wall.

Leap back up to the chamber's higher level and walk into the newly opened passageway. When you do, a booby trap is triggered and the room begins to transform around you as pillars jut out of the walls, threatening to crush you!

You emerge from the tunnel into a large chamber. As you enter, you sense that there is something dark inside, but before you can act, the Nightsister waiting high above the ground unleashes a powerful Force blast at the ceiling! Suddenly, the ceiling begins to crumble and give way. You try to run, but the floor cracks under your feet and gives way. You fall deep into the chamber foundation, and the ceiling falls on top of you. The Nightsister, pleased with her work, laughs and struts away. You're trapped.

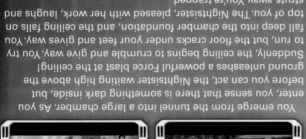

# RETURN TO CHRISTOPHSIS

As R2-D2, pass by the chatty battle droids and turn left up the hall.

**NOTE**

In this mission, you play as R2-D2 and C-3PO. There's no need to choose a Jedi pair.

to venture to the compound's main computer. There, the droids could get vital information.

The Jedi pair decide to split up with the droids, allowing them

Most of the Separatists were headed for that elevator. Good luck. As for me, I need to get

The Nightsister home planet of Dathomir proves as hostile as the witches, and the Jedi find themselves engaged in intense confrontation. Meanwhile, on Christophsis, the Council's investi-gation leads farther into the depths of the planet's core. As the two Jedi prepare to infiltrate the compound on Christophsis, Senator Amidala departs with the injured Commander Rex.

The compound looks like it extends much further. We need to get to the bottom of this soon.

We heard that one before. Move it before I blast you!

**TIP**

Halfway up the hall, turn left into the short hall and roll into the room at the far end. There is a Sith holocron here. Zap the two treadwell droids, claim the holocron for your own, and break open all the crates to find some Force orbs.

At the hall's end, you're met by two more battle droids that confuse you for a pair of new configuration droids and send you into the room behind them. In the room, you're tasked with configuring fresh battle droids and equipping them for war. Once you're alone in the room, you contact your Jedi Generals, who suggest you sabotage the droids by configuring them to be as least threatening as possible.

Break open the crates in the room, then begin your task by approaching the glowing console on the left. Activate the console and initiate the R2-D2 minigame. Match the colored notches in the spinning rings to the colored slots on the outer ring to complete the minigame successfully. After completing the R2-D2 minigame, a screen will flash showing the required piece of equipment for the battle droids. To sabotage them, use C-3PO to pick up useless items from the bins on the far right wall that are comparable in size to the ones onscreen; equip them on the droids. If the image is of a blaster rifle, equip the droids with the broom (the item in the first bin from the top). When the screen calls for a small blaster pistol, equip them with the drum item. When the image calls for a wrench, equip them with a spoon.

## NOTE

The R2-D2 console minigame will keep restarting if you fail. The C-3PO part of the puzzle cannot fail, so if C-3PO attempts to pick up the wrong item, R2-D2 will complain until the correct item is chosen.

## TRIVIA BOX

Plo Koon is Dave Filoni's (the director of the TV show) favorite Jedi.

After repeating the process three times and sabotaging the battle droids, the pair of droids that sent you into the room come storming back in with a new task for you.

Quiet! We've got something even a protocol droid can handle. Move!

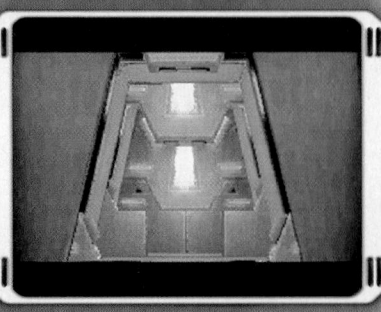

The bothersome battle droids escort you into a temperature-regulating room. In order to regulate the temperature of the large crystal in the room, you must stand on the two floor switches in front of the crystal. When your battle droid escorts leave you to your new task, Senator Amidala contacts you in need of information. She requests coordinates for a safe landing spot for Commander Gree. In the adjoining room is a computer console that R2-D2 can use to find such coordinates. Unfortunately, you're tied up in this room having to regulate the crystal's temperature. If you allow the crystal to overheat, the battle droids outside will rush into the room and fire at you.

The only way to access the computer in the adjoining room and not get caught is to roll onto one of the floor pressure switches in front of the crystal console. C-3PO will automatically step on the other pressure switch. This returns the crystal to a light blue color, which indicates its temperature is nominal. Immediately leave the pressure switch, and speed into one of the four small lit alcoves on the room's sides. This makes a panel retract and reveals a glowing console. Use the glowing console to complete the R2-D2 minigame, then rush back to the crystal console to raise the crystal's temperature before it turns red.

## CAUTION

If the reactor overheats for too long, the battle droids will return, causing the alcoves to reset!

Do this four times, one for each of the four alcoves in the room, to open the four sliding doors blocking the entrance to the adjoining room. Break all the crates in the room, grab the Force orbs and Ilum crystal, then dash into the adjoining room.

Grab the Sith holocron in the computer room, then use the computer console to complete the R2-D2 minigame. After completing it, you're able to grant Senator Amidala's request. Exit the room, back to the temperature-regulating room where you're confronted by two very irate battle droids.

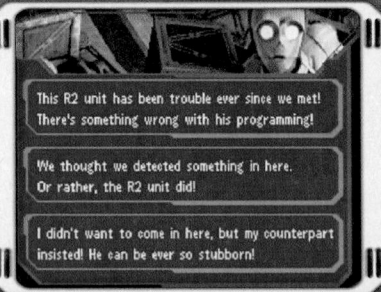

This R2 unit has been trouble ever since we met! There's something wrong with his programming!

We thought we detected something in here. Or rather, the R2 unit did!

I didn't want to come in here, but my counterpart insisted! He can be ever so stubborn!

When they ask why you weren't at your post, answer them with the following responses to avoid becoming a pile of junk parts.

"We thought we detected something in here. Or rather, the R2 unit did!"

"You're absolutely right! But he insisted something was awry!"

"Please don't! He was trying to remedy an error! Otherwise the whole system would have overloaded."

"He's no simple droid! Beneath those rusty dents is a truly remarkable exemplar of engineering finesse."

"R2-D2 detected a system malfunction! If he hadn't halted a failing process, we'd have been vaporized!"

Satisfied with your explanation, the two battle droids go back to their post. Just then, one of the Jedi Generals contacts you and requests that you open a factory door to create an escape route for him and his partner. While accessing the computer earlier, you spied another computer terminal nearby.

ine, just hurry. We're not sure how long we can hold [t]hem off!

**NOTE**

After the message from the Jedi General, you resume your adventure in a long hallway.

Head up the hall and turn left into the first small alcove. Activate the computer in the alcove to grant the Jedi's request. While accessing the computer, you also find plans for a new Separatist weapon! You report your findings to the Jedi Generals, then to the Jedi Council. The Jedi Generals send you to another computer terminal in case they need further help. Follow the hall up and enter the room at the end.

The room contains three colored consoles: one red, one yellow, and one blue. When you tap on one of the three colors, the console emits a high-, mid-, or low-pitched tone. Step into the area with the three consoles and wait for the main computer to emit the first set of tones. When they do, respond by pressing on the colored consoles to match the tones emitted by the main computer.

**TIP**

Watch the long vertical rows of colored lights along the far wall. As the main computer emits the sets of tones, the wall will light up with the matching color of the tones emitted from the main computer.

After completing the lights and sounds minigame, the door at the room's far end will open. Break the crates in the room before you go, and grab the Sith holocron near the center. Enter the newly opened door and roll north, into the hall.

As you strut into the next room, your Jedi counterparts are in another part of the complex being ambushed by battle droids! Suddenly, to make matters worse, you're being chased by a droid as well. You speed into the next room and shut the hatch behind you.

Shoot them, quick!

Activate the glowing console at the room's center. This initiates an R2-D2 lock puzzle. Complete it quickly and note the four symbols at the screen's bottom. After completing the puzzle as R2-D2, you take control of C-3PO.

As C-3PO, flip the switches along the wall in the same order as the symbols that appeared after completing the R2-D2 minigame. When you do, a large machine drops on the droids surrounding your Jedi friends, crushing them into little droid pancakes.

Your Jedi friends are saved! You slowly travel down the next hall and into a new chamber while the Jedi Generals infiltrate deep into the compound.

In the next room, break the containers to collect more Force orbs and an Ilum crystal, then use the glowing computer at the room's far left corner. Successfully complete the R2-D2 minigame and the first red light atop the far door turns blue. As C-3PO, activate the glowing console on the room's far right corner and successfully complete the symbol-matching minigame. When you do, the second red light turns blue.

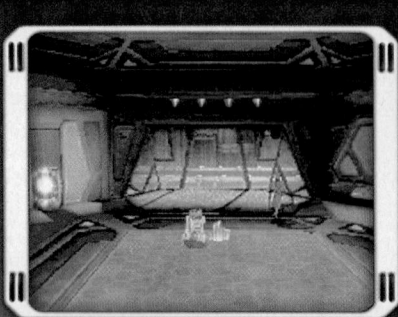

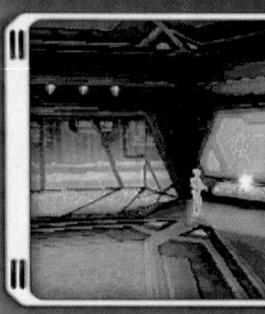

Continue switching back and forth between the two droids, completing console minigames until all four red lights are blue and the door unlocks.

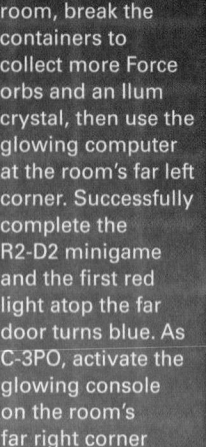

## NOTE

The minigames increase in difficulty as you bounce back and forth between them.

Your efforts pay off, and the Jedi pair press on deeper into the compound. As they speed along, destroying droids as they go, they're interrupted by none other than Count Dooku! The Jedi inform Dooku that as they speak, the location of his secret weapon, the Separatist Battle Station, is being sent to the Jedi Council.

Beautiful, isn't it. Such a pure physical manifestation of the Force's majesty and might.

The Jedi draw their lightsabers, but Dooku acts quickly! He distracts them with a surge of Sith lightning and escapes....

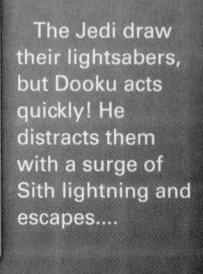

## TRIVIA BOX

There are 30 possible playable combinations of Jedi for each mission.

# RETURN TO DATHOMIR

The confrontation with Dooku on Christophsis comes with the horrific revelation of the Separatist's latest weapon, a battleship weaponry system powered by the Force. With the dissemination of this information across all Jedi Council members, the mission of the Jedi on Dathomir takes on a much graver urgency. Back on Dathomir, the two Jedi sent to investigate emerge from their rubble prison with only a few bumps and bruises.

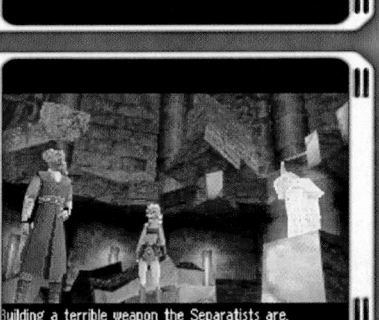

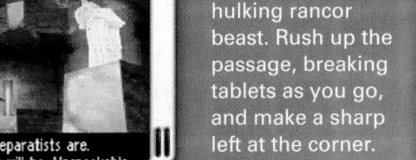

Building a terrible weapon the Separatists are. powered by the stolen crystals it will be. Unspeakable.

As you recover from your temporary tomb, you receive a holo-transmission from Master Yoda. He informs you about the Force-powered Separatist weapon.

consequences on the Force this act will have.

Most frightening of all is Yoda's sudden revelation that the Nightsisters must be charging the crystals harvested from Dathomir, Christophsis, and Rodia. Your mission is clear—stop the Nightsisters!

**NOTE**

You resume the mission on Dathomir with the Jedi you chose for the sixth mission. We chose Plo Koon and Ahsoka Tano for the sixth mission, so we assume control over them once again.

As the primary Jedi, resume your mission on Dathomir by first breaking all the tablets nearby and collecting the Force orbs. Exit the chamber through the passageway on the far wall.

Look out!

In the next chamber, a small stormtrooper squadron is engaged with a hulking rancor beast. Rush up the passage, breaking tablets as you go, and make a sharp left at the corner. The rancor beast sees you and gives chase.

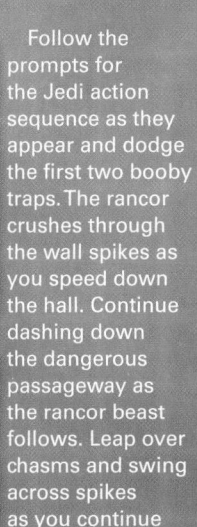

Follow the prompts for the Jedi action sequence as they appear and dodge the first two booby traps. The rancor crushes through the wall spikes as you speed down the hall. Continue dashing down the dangerous passageway as the rancor beast follows. Leap over chasms and swing across spikes as you continue following the Jedi action sequence prompts. When you reach the chasm's opposite end, the

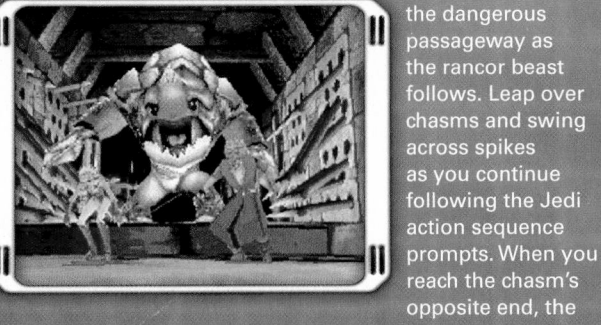

rancor beast fails to make it all the way across, and your lose the bothersome beast.

As the secondary Jedi, run into the room and flip the first glowing switch. When it deactivates the force field on the level below, you can run down the walkway as the primary Jedi and flip the switch on the bottom level. Continue switching back and forth between the two Jedi as you drop force fields and slowly move forward.

When you reach the walkway's end, leap from beam to beam as they pop in and out of the wall, and storm across the long chasm.

At the next chasm, wait for the pillars to jut out of the ground. As soon as they do, leap onto the first one and press the glowing switch to drop the force field for your partner above you. Then use the next pillar to jump across the chasm to safety.

Round the next corner and jump onto the ledge high above you, reuniting with your partner. Wait for the force fields ahead to drop, then carefully speed past each one. When you reach the end, you find yourself back in the main room where the Nightsisters ambushed you. There are two large spinning wheels that open a large stone door at the center. This time, step on the two floor switches on the room's right side.

Break the tablets on the chasm's other side, then tap on the glowing switch by the door to open it up.

Immediately upon entering the next room, you're ambushed by a group of Nightsisters. Focus on the dark Nightsisters first, then eliminate the red Nightsisters. With the foes eliminated, step on the floor switch on the room's left side. When you do, the nearby door will slide open, and your secondary Jedi will automatically leap onto the stepped doorways and climb up to the chamber's second level.

## TRIVIA BOX

Nightsisters use a modified version of the lightsaber design. The long swords have an additional two-prong fork at the hilt. The Nightsisters also use a short-sword variant.

As the primary Jedi, walk into the newly opened room and step on the floor switch on the walkway's right. This slides open the door for your partner, allowing him or her access into the upper level.

Enter the long, ribbed hallway.

Make a left into the next section of the long winding chamber. Follow the walkway up, then left again, breaking spires as you go, until you reach a tall stepped wall. Break the tablets on both sides of the wall, then leap up the steps until you're on the chamber's next level. You emerge back in the main room once again, but this time, the second large wheel lifts the final stone door and reveals a passage deeper into the compound.

Crush the Night-sisters in the room, then break open the tablets and spires nearby to collect more Force orbs.

Rush onto the bridge in the next room and engage the blue Night-sisters. Destroy them as you move across all the bridge's crossing sections. Break open the small spires on the bridge to find Force orbs and two Ilum crystals. After defeating all the Nightsisters on the bridge, turn left onto the left crossing section and step on the two floor switches flanking the doorway. Dash through the door when it opens, and storm deeper into the compound.

Destroy the stone tablets and spires as you rush up the orange-hued hall, and collect all the Force orbs they release. Follow the hall to its end, where you reach a large chamber. There, a group of Nightsisters drops in on you and attacks! Fend off the feisty sisters. During battle, one of the blue Night-sisters unleashes a Force attack on you that sends you flying through a wall.

On the wall's other side, you find yourself in a long chamber with a series of precarious broken walkways stretching across a long chasm. One of the Nightsisters struts into the room with you and challenges you to a fight. She's not a part of your mission, yet, so instead you decide to leap across the chasm.

**TIP**

While in the long hallway, examine the east wall. There is an ornate, secret doorway that you can open with a Team Up Environmental ability with two environment Jedi. A collectible Sith holocron is within the secret chamber.

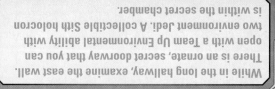

Follow the onscreen Jedi action sequence prompts to leap across the crumbling walkways. While you leap and swing across the crumbling walkways, the Nightsister uses the Force to bring the rest of the room crumbling down around you.

Upon reaching the chasm's other side, a clone trooper battalion drops in and provides cover fire from the Night-sister's attacks!

Rush around the stasis pillars and strike the glowing pillars. If they are surrounded by a red force field, move on to the next glowing pillar.

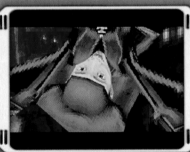

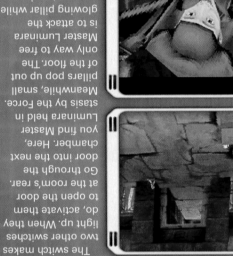

Master Luminara is to attack the glowing pillar while your partner jumps on one of the other pillars.

The switch makes two other switches light up. When they do, activate them to open the door at the room's rear. Go through the door into the next chamber. Here, you find Master Luminara held in stasis by the Force. Meanwhile, small pillars pop up out of the floor. The only way to free Master Luminara is to attack the glowing pillar while your partner jumps on one of the other pillars.

Rush to the back of the chamber and activate the glowing switch.

**TRIVIA BOX**

**Over 200 concept art pieces were created for the game. Some of this concept art can be unlocked and viewed in the Extras menu.**

After checking on Master Luminara, rush after the cowardly Nightsister. You finally catch her, pinned by your clone troopers' fire. Engage her in battle and use combos to fill your Team Up Combo meter. Once the meter is full, unleash a Team Up Combo to slice off a huge chunk of her health. Dodge her Force blast, then counter with quick combos.

After taking a bit of damage, Sai Sircu flees again. This time she cuts the chains holding up the chamber door and slows you down. On the door's other side, Sai Sircu sends a communication stating that the crystals are charged and ready for transport to the Devastation starship.

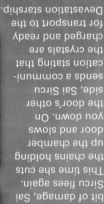

After you destroy all four pillars, Master Luminara is released and falls to the ground. When this happens, the Nightsister boss, Sai Sircu, jumps down and confronts you. The Nightsister temporarily escapes while you check to see if Master Luminara is okay.

# THE DEVASTATION

As the Jedi set off to stop the Separatist battle cruiser, the Devastation, Yoda presses upon them the urgency of succeeding in their mission. However, unbeknownst to anyone, the uneasy alliance between Dooku's Separatist forces and the Nightsisters takes an unexpected turn. After the crystals from the planets Christophsis and Dathomir have been installed into the battle cruiser's main weapon chamber, only the Rodian crystals are missing.

In spite of the Rodian crystals being missing, the Nightsister is confident that she can boost the power of the Dathomir crystals. Lord Sidious conveys his disappointment through the holo-communication device, but Count Dooku is confident that the weapon is actually more powerful than expected, despite the missing crystals.

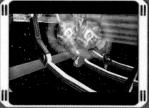

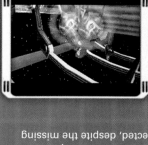
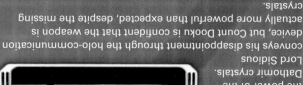

Asajj Ventress suggests that they demonstrate the weapon's power to Lord Sidious. He likes the suggestion and orders Dooku to set course for Dathomir. While Ventress sets the coordinates to the Nightsister home planet, Sai Sircu takes exception to Sidious's suggested target and she quietly sneaks away. As she does, she charges her Force powers, then unleashes a Force blast on both Dooku and Ventress!

**NOTE**

At this point, you take control of the first pair of Jedi. Throughout the mission, you will control the entire cast of Jedi by leading different pairs into battle.

Meanwhile, back at the Jedi Council chamber on Coruscant, the Council convenes from across the galaxy via holo-communication. Yoda, the only one actually in the Council chamber, stresses the importance of stopping the Devastation. The various Jedi are paired up and prepare to launch an all-out assault on the Devastation. This is their only hope.....

**TRIVIA BOX**

The game features a scene with the Jedi being chased by a rancor. The rancor is indigenous to Dathomir, the home of the Nightsisters.

Sai Sircu knocks the dastardly duo into a separate chamber of the Devastation's bridge and locks them out. She then redirects the Devastation toward Coruscant.

You arrive at the Devastation via starfighter and rush into the cruiser's landing bay, where you're greeted by a battalion of super battle droids! Reflect their fire back at them, or deflect their blaster fire away as you approach them and get within 'saber range. After destroying the super battle droids, a group of Magna guards rushes into battle. Take them out with a few quick strikes of your 'saber and clear the hangar bay of all enemies.

Hold your position and reflect the turrets' blaster fire back at them. If you can't reflect the turrets' fire, then sprint up to them and destroy them with the Force. After demolishing the turrets, turn your attention to the attacking droids. Once the room is clear of enemies, crush open the crates to collect more Force orbs. Flip the two switches by the door at the far end, then enter the passage into the new area.

Before leaving the hangar bay, break all the containers in it to find some Force orbs.

In the next corridor, approach the red force field and disable it by cutting through the white beams next to it.

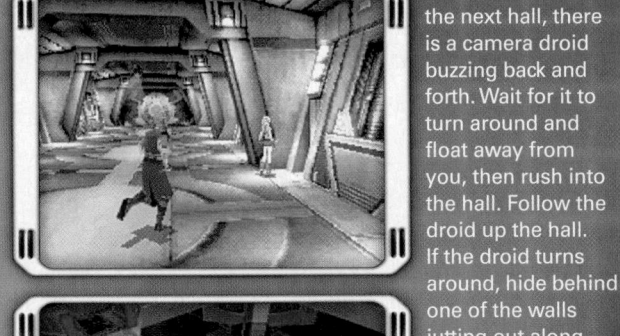

Run up to the hangar's far end and hop on the small platform along the right wall. Press the red button on the platform, and ride it up to the second level. When you reach the second level, a group of battle droids enter through a nearby door. Rush the droids and chop them up.

Press the glowing consoles flanking the door along the far wall, then head into the corridor. Grab the Ilum crystal as you go, then enter the room at the hall's end, which houses two large turrets and several droids.

Farther down the next hall, there is a camera droid buzzing back and forth. Wait for it to turn around and float away from you, then rush into the hall. Follow the droid up the hall. If the droid turns around, hide behind one of the walls jutting out along the corridor and let it pass you by.

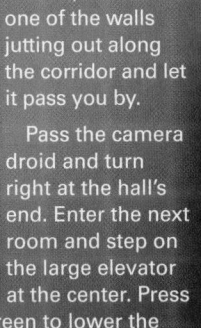

Pass the camera droid and turn right at the hall's end. Enter the next room and step on the large elevator at the center. Press left, left, down, then down again on the screen to lower the elevator to the proper floor and exit.

Step off the lift and enter the next hallway. Break the containers as you storm up the hall, and collect the Force orbs and Ilum crystal.

About halfway up the hall, you're attacked by several buzz droids. Rush the rotund robots and run your lightsaber through them. Attack with quick combos and leap from droid to droid as you demolish them.

Rush right, into the corridor from where the droids appeared, and crack the containers open. Collect more Force orbs, then run to the hall's end.

In the next room, you're greeted by Asajj Ventress. To defeat Ventress, don't engage her directly. In fact, your priority isn't Ventress but the power grid on this section of the ship. When the battle begins, destroy a battle droid, then Force Throw it at Ventress to stun her. While she is stunned, run to the bridge's north section and activate one of the glowing consoles. The switch lowers the floor, exposing part of the power grid. Destroy the power grids by repeatedly slashing them, then return to the fight against Ventress.

Repeat the process two more times for the other power grids, and leave the hand-to-hand battle against Ventress to your partner. Once all three power grids have been destroyed, Ventress accidentally hints at a backup power grid elsewhere on the ship.

Crush the battle droids on the second level, then activate the two glowing switches along the north wall. A passage opens up, granting you entry into the next corridor.

Meanwhile, elsewhere on the ship, a second pair of Jedi land on the Devastation. As the new primary Jedi, attack the Magna guards as they rush into the hangar. While you engage the Magna guards, a group of battle droids opens fire from a nearby turret. Either reflect the turret's fire back at it, or Force Throw crates at it and destroy it. Step on the platform at the hangar's north end and ride it to the top level.

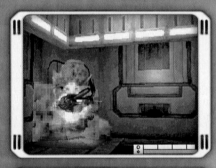

Before you can resume the battle against Ventress, Sai Sircu arrives and attacks the bald-headed baddy!

---

In the next room, you find the ship's reactor core. It is flanked by two doors leading into smaller rooms and guarded by two camera droids. While avoiding the camera droids, dash into the right corridor. Walk to the end and tap on the glowing console. Complete the symbol-matching minigame to partially activate the console in the reactor room.

Return to the reactor room, but this time, sneak past the camera droid on the left and into the left room. The console in this room has three levers. Pull on them in the following order—left, middle, middle so that the colors above them match what is displayed on the wall. The console in the main reactor room lights up, and the computer console becomes active.

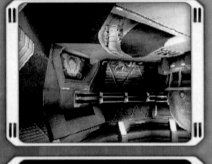

**TIP**

At the end of this hall, before turning right, is a room covered by several stacked crates. Use a Team Up Environmental ability with an environmental and combat Jedi to find another Sith holocron.

In the next hall, sever the white beam to bring down the red force field. Creep up the corridor and hide behind the large barrels to avoid being detected by the camera droid buzzing by. Quickly defeat any buzz droids that appear, then press the glowing button on the right wall. The camera droid buzzes away, and the next red force field deactivates. Sneak past another camera droid and turn right at the hall's end.

Return to the reactor room and sneak past the camera droids again, toward the main computer. Activate the computer to overload the reactor, then get some cover behind the large barricade at the room's rear.

Walk to the hall's far end and enter the room there. You find Count Dooku talking to Darth Sidious via holo-communication. The traitorous Sith Lords are angered by Sai Sircu's betrayal. During their discussion, you hear Dooku mention the battle cruiser's new target—Coruscant! You rush in with your 'saber ready for battle!

should have expected such betrayal from a nightsister witch

### CAUTION

If you're caught by the camera droids, it'll summon several Magna guards to attack!

When the reactor explodes, it reveals a passage behind it. Defeat the battle droids that spill out of the passage, then grab the Ilum crystal on the room's far right corner. Break open the crates nearby to collect more Force orbs, then saunter into the passage. Follow the corridor to its end, collecting more Force orbs as you go, then get on the lift. Press right, then down to move the lift into position, and enter the next corridor.

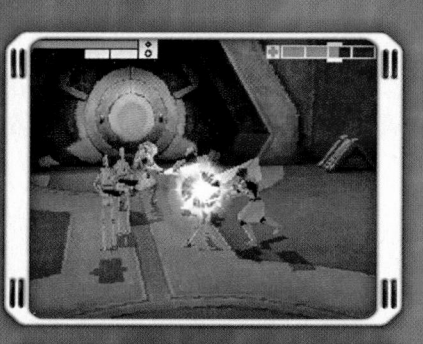

Like the recent battle with Ventress, during the battle against Dooku, the villain is not your priority. Instead, destroy the six targeting consoles on the upper level. Avoid direct combat with Dooku—that is for another episode. Instead, destroy the battle droids that join the fight, and throw them at the Count.

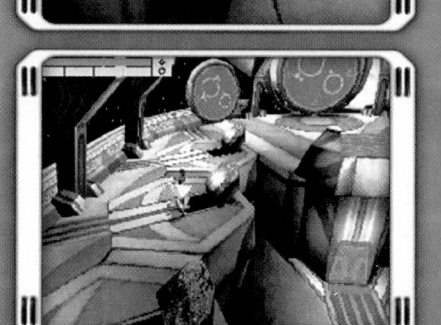

While he is stunned, jump up to the higher level and destroy one of the six glowing consoles. Repeat the process five more times until all six targeting consoles are destroyed.

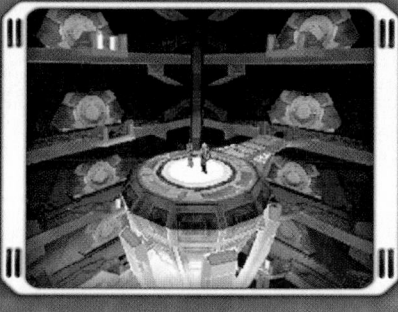

Walk up the corridor, breaking more containers as you go, and destroy the buzz droids in your way.

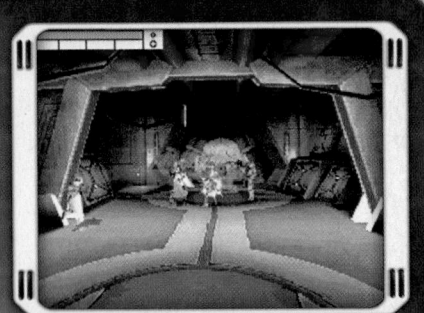

Destroy the droids at the hall's end and trundle into the next section of the hall. As you enter, you can sense a dark force nearby. Follow the hall to the bend and turn right. Enter the elevator room at the hall's end and hop on the lift. Press left twice, then up twice to reach your destination. Get off the lift.

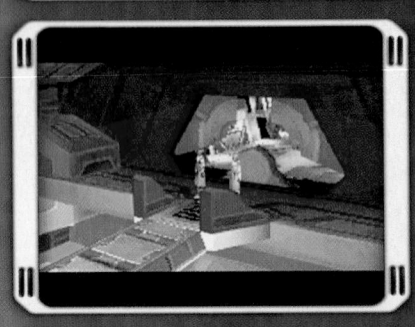

In the next hall, you're greeted by several more buzz droids. Instead of staying and fighting, however, you sneak into a ventilation shaft. Follow the onscreen Jedi action sequence prompts to leap across the long shaft and destroy the droids on the other side. Continue following the prompts to leap from security droid to security droid. Climb up the tall shaft and onto an entryway back into the facility.

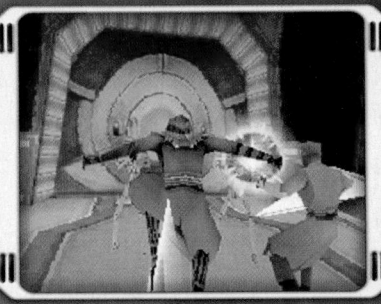

### CAUTION

If you take too long in jumping up to the higher level or destroying the console after stunning Dooku, he'll regain his balance and knock you down from the higher level.

After you destroy the consoles, Sai Sircu joins the fight. She hits you and Dooku with a powerful Force blast that knocks you out. In the attack, Dooku flees and she gets away.

With the second pair of Jedi knocked unconscious, the hopes of the mission rest on the third pair of Jedi on the Devastation. As they land in the hangar bay, they are met by Magna guards. As the new primary Jedi, attack the Magna guard and dispatch them quickly.

Rush through the rear hangar door into a large storage room and break open the crates inside. Turn left and walk past the malfunctioning force fields. Wait for the fields to deactivate, then rush past them. Grab the Ilum crystal on the left as you go.

### TIP

At the end of this hall, before turning right at the corner, use a Team Up Environmental ability with two combat Jedi to break through a cracked wall and find another Sith holocron.

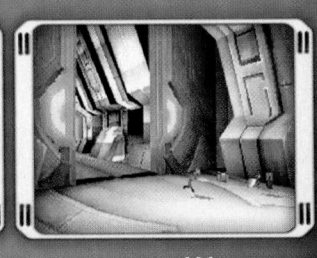

Back inside the facility, you're met by a group of Magna guards. Cut your way past them to the opposite side of the large room. Break open the crates and collect the Ilum crystals on the ground.

Run into the next room and confront Sai Sircu. There, you find Sai Sircu perched high above the ground atop a tall ledge. She greets you with a Force blast that almost knocks you off your feet. She's itching for a battle and quickly attacks from a platform above you. Between you and her, there is a force field that turns on and off.

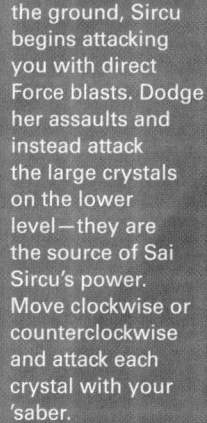

Along the room's sides, crates periodically trickle down the wall from a conveyor belt. When the battle begins, use the Force to throw crates at Sai Sircu while the force field is not active. The crates will hit one of the four supporting beams on her platform and destroy it.

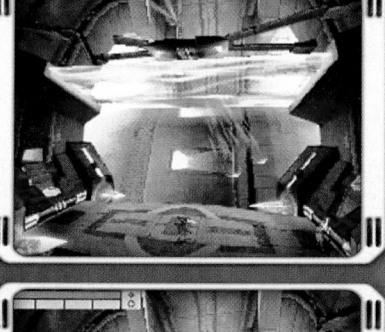

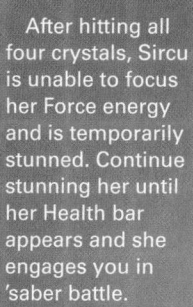

Once she's on the ground, Sircu begins attacking you with direct Force blasts. Dodge her assaults and instead attack the large crystals on the lower level—they are the source of Sai Sircu's power. Move clockwise or counterclockwise and attack each crystal with your 'saber.

After hitting all four crystals, Sircu is unable to focus her Force energy and is temporarily stunned. Continue stunning her until her Health bar appears and she engages you in 'saber battle.

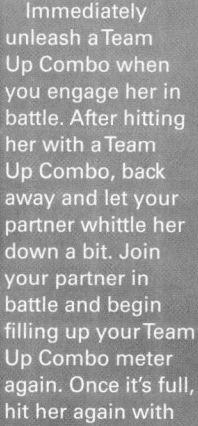

Dodge Sai Sircu's Force blasts while you pepper her platform with crates until you destroy all four support beams.

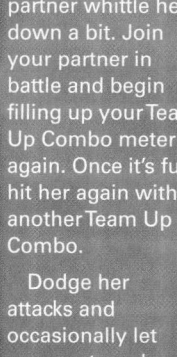

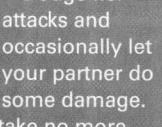

Immediately unleash a Team Up Combo when you engage her in battle. After hitting her with a Team Up Combo, back away and let your partner whittle her down a bit. Join your partner in battle and begin filling up your Team Up Combo meter again. Once it's full, hit her again with another Team Up Combo.

Dodge her attacks and occasionally let your partner do some damage. After a few more exchanges, Sai Sircu can take no more.

## TIP

Watch the sides for falling objects. When they fall, use the Force to throw them at her!

## TRIVIA BOX

The development team is truly multinational with over 15 countries represented.

Once she's sustained too much damage, Sai Sircu backs away and falls to her knees. The energy beam surrounds her and slowly lifts her into the air. The Force energy flows from her to the four surrounding crystals and quickly amplifies!

Suddenly, in a beam of light, Sai Sircu is joined with the Force... permanently. The Jedi all rush to their starfighters and escape the Devastation just as the large battle cruiser explodes!

# UNLOCKABLES

The following secret Jedi scrolls were found among the many ruins that remained after the Clone Wars. They detail information on how to unlock all pieces of concept art, costume, and other unlockables in *Star Wars: The Clone Wars—Jedi Alliance*.

| How to Get It | Description |
| --- | --- |
| Defeat 100 total enemies in Coruscant Mission 1 | Unlocks Coruscant 4 concept art in the Extras screen |
| Defeat 100 total enemies in Rodia Mission 1 | Unlocks Sedawan 3 concept art in the Extras screen |
| Defeat 100 total enemies in Sedawan | Unlocks Sedawan 1 concept art in the Extras screen |
| Complete Devastation | Unlocks Devastation 9 concept art in the Extras screen |
| Complete Dathomir Mission 2 | Unlocks Dathomir 10 concept art in the Extras screen |
| Complete Christophsis Mission 2 | Unlocks Christophsis 7 concept art in the Extras screen |
| Complete Dathomir Mission 1 | Unlocks Dathomir 3 concept art in the Extras screen |
| Complete Christophsis Mission 1 | Unlocks Christophsis 3 concept art in the Extras screen |
| Complete Rodia Mission 2 | Unlocks Coruscant 1 concept art in the Extras screen |
| Complete Coruscant Mission 1 | Unlocks Coruscant 2 concept art in the Extras screen |
| Complete Rodia Mission 1 | Unlocks Sedawan 4 concept art in the Extras screen |
| Complete Sedawan | Unlocks Sedawan 2 concept art in the Extras screen |
| Complete a chain by killing 5 enemies in a row in Devastation | Unlocks model of a clone in the Extras screen |
| Complete a chain by killing 5 enemies in a row in Dathomir Mission 2 | Unlocks model of Obi-Wan Kenobi in the Extras screen |
| Complete a chain by killing 5 enemies in a row in Christophsis Mission 2 | Unlocks model of Kit Fisto in the Extras screen |
| Complete a chain by killing 5 enemies in a row in Dathomir Mission 1 | Unlocks model of Plo Koon in the Extras screen |
| Complete a chain by killing 5 enemies in a row in Christophsis Mission 1 | Unlocks model of Mace Windu in the Extras screen |
| Complete a chain by killing 5 enemies in a row in Rodia Mission 2 | Unlocks model of R2-D2 in the Extras screen |
| Complete a chain by killing 5 enemies in a row in Coruscant Mission 1 | Unlocks model of C-3PO in the Extras screen |
| Complete a chain by killing 5 enemies in a row in Rodia Mission 1 | Unlocks model of Anakin Skywalker in the Extras screen |
| Complete a chain by killing 5 enemies in a row in Sedawan | Unlocks model of Ahsoka Tano in the Extras screen |
| Collect all 3 Sith holocrons in Devastation | Unlocks model of Count Dooku in the Extras screen |
| Collect all 3 Sith holocrons in Dathomir Mission 2 | Unlocks model of Sai Sircu in the Extras screen |
| Collect all 3 Sith holocrons in Christophsis Mission 2 | Unlocks model of rancor in the Extras screen |
| Collect all 3 Sith holocrons in Dathomir Mission 1 | Unlocks model of Padmé Amidala in the Extras screen |
| Collect all 3 Sith holocrons in Christophsis Mission 1 | Unlocks model of boss miner droid in the Extras screen |
| Collect all 3 Sith holocrons in Rodia Mission 3 | Unlocks model of Nightsister 2 in the Extras screen |
| Collect all 3 Sith holocrons in Coruscant Mission 1 | Unlocks model of Nightsister 1 in the Extras screen |
| Collect all 3 Sith holocrons in Rodia Mission 1 | Unlocks model of the gunship in the Extras screen |
| Collect all 3 Sith holocrons in Sedawan | Unlocks model of Commander Cody in the Extras screen |
| Collect all Ilum crystals in Devastation | Unlocks model of Darth Sidious in the Extras screen |
| Collect all Ilum crystals in Dathomir Mission 2 | Unlocks model of miner droid in the Extras screen |
| Collect all Ilum crystals in Christophsis Mission 2 | Unlocks model of Magna guard in the Extras screen |
| Collect all Ilum crystals in Dathomir Mission 1 | Unlocks model of Luminara in the Extras screen |
| Collect all Ilum crystals in Christophsis Mission 1 | Unlocks model of camera droid in the Extras screen |
| Collect all Ilum crystals in Rodia Mission 2 | Unlocks model of Ziro the Hutt in the Extras screen |
| Collect all Ilum crystals in Coruscant Mission 1 | Unlocks model of super buzz droid in the Extras screen |
| Collect all Ilum crystals in Rodia Mission 1 | Unlocks model of buzz droid in the Extras screen |
| Collect all Ilum crystals in Sedawan | Unlocks model of battle droid in the Extras screen |
| Collect all Force orbs in Devastation | Unlocks 2nd bonus costume for Ahsoka |
| Collect all Force orbs in Dathomir Mission 2 | Unlocks 2nd bonus costume for Obi-Wan |
| Collect all Force orbs in Christophsis Mission 2 | Unlocks 2nd bonus costume for Anakin |
| Collect all Force orbs in Dathomir Mission 1 | Unlocks bonus costume for Obi-Wan |
| Collect all Force orbs in Christophsis Mission 1 | Unlocks bonus costume for Mace Windu |
| Collect all Force orbs in Rodia Mission 2 | Unlocks bonus costume for Kit Fisto |
| Collect all Force orbs in Coruscant Mission 1 | Unlocks bonus costume for Plo Koon |
| Collect all Force orbs in Rodia Mission 1 | Unlocks bonus costume for Ahsoka |
| Collect all Force orbs in Sedawan | Unlocks bonus costume for Anakin |

STAR WARS THE CLONE WARS — JEDI ALLIANCE

| How to Get It | Description |
|---|---|
| Defeat 100 total enemies in Rodia Mission 2 | Unlocks Coruscant 3 concept art in the Extras screen |
| Defeat 100 total enemies in Christophsis Mission 1 | Unlocks Christophsis 1 concept art in the Extras screen |
| Defeat 100 total enemies in Dathomir Mission 1 | Unlocks Dathomir 1 concept art in the Extras screen |
| Defeat 100 total enemies in Christophsis Mission 2 | Unlocks Christophsis 8 concept art in the Extras screen |
| Defeat 100 total enemies in Dathomir Mission 2 | Unlocks Dathomir 11 concept art in the Extras screen |
| Defeat 100 total enemies in Devastation | Unlocks Devastation 12 concept art in the Extras screen |
| Complete Sedawan | Unlocks Jedi bomber concept art in the Extras screen |
| Complete Rodia Mission 1 | Unlocks the Sedawan 1 concept art in the Extras screen |
| Complete Coruscant Mission 1 | Unlocks Coruscant vehicles concept art in the Extras screen |
| Complete Rodia Mission 2 | Unlocks Rodia train concept art in the Extras screen |
| Complete Christophsis Mission 1 | Unlocks miner droid concept art in the Extras screen |
| Complete Dathomir Mission 1 | Unlocks super buzz droid concept art in the Extras screen |
| Complete Christophsis Mission 2 | Unlocks Nightsister 2A concept art in the Extras screen |
| Complete Dathomir Mission 2 | Unlocks super miner droid 2 concept art in the Extras screen |
| Complete Devastation | Unlocks Nightsister transport ship concept art in the Extras screen |
| Finish Sedawan without picking up any items | Unlocks Concept Art 2 in the Extras screen |
| Finish Rodia Mission 1 without picking up any items | Unlocks Concept Art 16 in the Extras screen |
| Finish Coruscant Mission 1 without picking up any items | Unlocks Concept Art 1 in the Extras screen |
| Finish Rodia Mission 2 without picking up any items | Unlocks Concept Art 4 in the Extras screen |
| Finish Christophsis Mission 1 without picking up any items | Unlocks Concept Art 8 in the Extras screen |
| Finish Dathomir Mission 1 without picking up any items | Unlocks Concept Art 7 in the Extras screen |
| Finish Christophsis Mission 2 without picking up any items | Unlocks Concept Art 6 in the Extras screen |
| Finish Dathomir Mission 2 without picking up any items | Unlocks Concept Art 9 in the Extras screen |
| Finish Devastation without picking up any items | Unlocks Concept Art 17 in the Extras screen |
| Complete Sedawan without losing all your health | Unlocks Devastation 2 concept art in the Extras screen |
| Complete Rodia Mission 1 without losing all your health | Unlocks Christophsis 5 concept art in the Extras screen |
| Complete Coruscant Mission 1 without losing all your health | Unlocks Christophsis 4 concept art in the Extras screen |
| Complete Rodia Mission 2 without losing all your health | Unlocks Christophsis 6 concept art in the Extras screen |
| Complete Christophsis Mission 1 without losing all your health | Unlocks Dathomir 8 concept art in the Extras screen |
| Complete Dathomir Mission 1 without losing all your health | Unlocks Dathomir 9 concept art in the Extras screen |
| Complete Christophsis Mission 2 without losing all your health | Unlocks Devastation 13 concept art in the Extras screen |
| Complete Dathomir Mission 2 without losing all your health | Unlocks Sedawan 6 concept art in the Extras screen |
| Complete Sedawan without losing all your health | Unlocks Dathomir 7 concept art in the Extras screen |
| Complete Sedawan with all pairings | Unlocks Concept Art 3 in the Extras screen |
| Complete Rodia Mission 1 with all pairings | Unlocks Concept Art 5 in the Extras screen |
| Complete Coruscant Mission 1 with all pairings | Unlocks Concept Art 10 in the Extras screen |
| Complete Rodia Mission 2 with all pairings | Unlocks Concept Art 11 in the Extras screen |
| Complete Christophsis Mission 1 with all pairings | Unlocks Concept Art 12 in the Extras screen |
| Complete Dathomir Mission 1 with all pairings | Unlocks Concept Art 13 in the Extras screen |
| Complete Christophsis Mission 2 with all pairings | Unlocks Concept Art 14 in the Extras screen |
| Complete Dathomir Mission 2 with all pairings | Unlocks Concept Art 15 in the Extras screen |
| Complete Devastation with all pairings | Unlocks Devastation 2 concept art in the Extras screen |
| Defeat all enemies in Sedawan | Unlock Super Enemies tweak in the Extras screen. Your enemies will be stronger. |
| Defeat all enemies in Rodia Mission 1 | Unlock Super Lightsaber tweak in the Extras screen. Your lightsaber will be more powerful. |
| Defeat all enemies in Coruscant Mission 1 | Unlock Super Team Up Combat tweak in the Extras screen. Double the rate you acquire Force energy. |
| Defeat all enemies in Rodia Mission 2 | Unlock Super Block tweak in the Extras screen. Double the stopping power of your block. |
| Defeat all enemies in Christophsis Mission 1 | Unlock Super Force Attack tweak in the Extras screen. A single Force attack defeats enemies. |
| Defeat all enemies in Dathomir Mission 1 | Unlock Auto Laser Deflect tweak in the Extras screen. Automatically deflect lasers back at their source. |
| Defeat all enemies in Christophsis Mission 2 | Unlock Extended Chain tweak in the Extras screen. You'll have more time to continue your chain. |
| Defeat all enemies in Dathomir Mission 2 | Unlock Health Restore tweak in the Extras screen. Instantly recover all your health after combat. |
| Defeat all enemies in Devastation | Unlock Immortality tweak in the Extras screen. You're immune to all but the Power Off button. |

CONCEPT ART

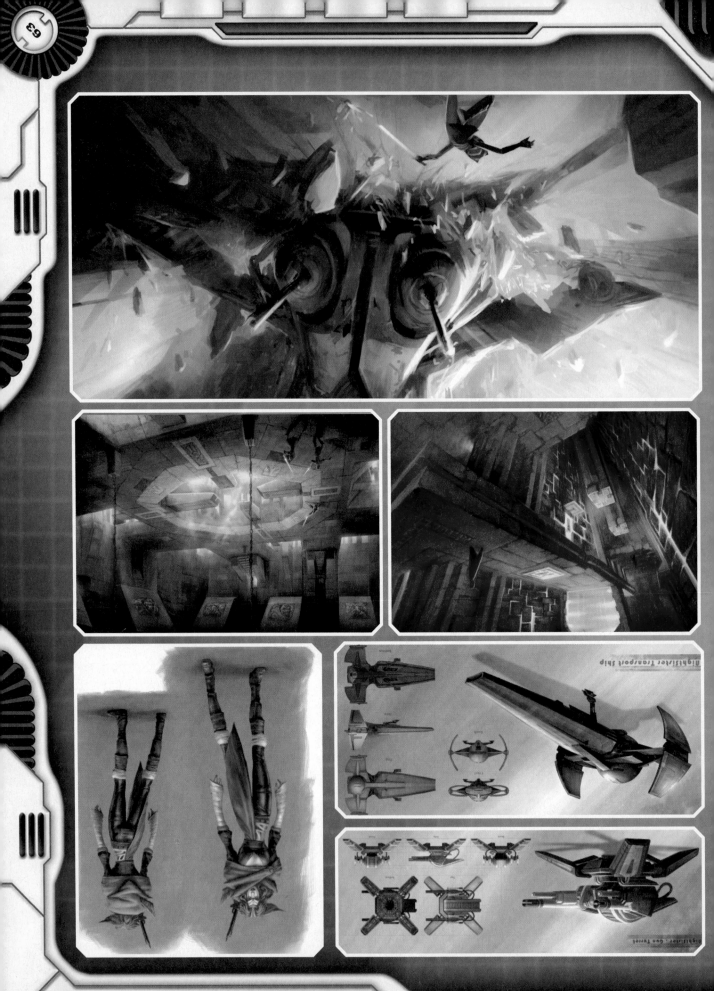

Nightstalker transport ship

Nightstalker Gun Turret

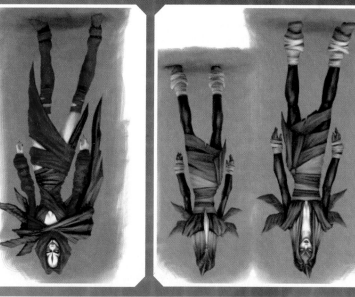